"Football Town"

A story about a small rural community,
Their school,
&
Their football team

Shades Creek Press, LLC
Savannah, Georgia

ISBN 978-0-615-47261-4

Jesse R. Hale

ACKNOWLEDGEMENTS

I would like to express my thanks and appreciation for all those who lent their support, gave their love, and tolerated my obsession to get this project published.

To all those who participated in this project many years ago, I extend a special thanks and sincere expression of appreciation. It goes without saying that, without you, and there are too many to name here, this project would have never been born.

Finally, to those we have lost, who were members of our school and community family, they are missed.

Note to the Reader:

As the author and creator of this book, I want to thank you for taking the time and effort to read it. It is a compilation of many years of study and research about small rural communities and the people and schools within these small settings. The stories recorded here are actual events. The emotions expressed by those who participated are real emotions. Some of the stories are funny, some are sad or troubling; but, they are a reflection of the people of Bainesville's heart and soul.

So, read with care.

Jesse R. Hale

Disclaimer

This book is in part a product of research and non-fiction. The stories are recorded as they were told to me, some verbatim, out of respect for all those who were interviewed or provided comment. All requirements were met prior to the research and interviews, in accordance with the standards and requirements prescribed by Vanderbilt University. The names used are pseudonyms. Some the story details have been changed slightly so not to reveal exact details of identity, although some situations as reported and retold by parents, students, community members, or from the local newspaper, were recounted as they were recorded during the interview and data gathering process.

Copyright 2011, Jesse R. Hale
ISBN 978-0-615-47261-4

Published by Shades Creek Press, LLC
Savannah, Georgia
www.shadescreekpress.com

DEDICATIONS

This book is dedicated to the memory of those members of the Bainesville High School community and family who are no longer on this earth. We are all better for having known them.

Dawn
Sam
Michelle

Contents

Introduction

In the spring of 1994, I was granted admission to the Peabody College of Teaching and Learning at Vanderbilt University, as a member of the fall, 1994, cohort for the doctoral program. This marked a pivotal time in my life, in that completing the program would require travel from Atlanta to Nashville, cooperation from my new employer as I entered into my first school administrative job as a middle school assistant principal, and support from my wife and family. The program was at a different level of complexity and challenge than I had faced or experienced previously. There was a great deal of trepidation as I summoned my best degree of self-confidence, which in its infant stages, I believed was more like blind faith in oneself to persevere and forge ahead, if only one step at a time.

The first night of class was intimidating. There were approximately 60 students in the class from all parts of the country and the world and from a variety of colleges and universities. It was, indeed, a heady group. I felt under-qualified to be there, but buckled up for the ride; I was in the program as an official member of this cohort. As the night progressed, the class discussion was designed to put everyone at ease, lay the ground rules, and of course, discuss the first assignment that had been mailed to each student prior to class. The level of thought and intellectual analysis required for the assignments was much more than required for the courses I had taken at the University of Georgia and elsewhere. I quickly realized that I was like a sponge, soaking up every minute of discussion.

After class, a group of about 12 of us went to dinner together, gathering at a place called the Cookery. This first class and first meal began the forming and bonding of friendships that still exist today. The Peabody experience was a life-changing journey.

During the second summer of classes, we were required to write our proposal for our doctoral research and study, which would eventually be molded into a dissertation. I was captivated by the aspect of organizational culture, traditions, ethos, myths, and folklore. I was also interested in the mythical power of southern football, specifically the rivalry in the State of Alabama between the University of Alabama and Auburn University. It is a rivalry that has existed for more than 100 years, and can divide a household, hold up a marriage, or dominate the colors adorned by their fans. The curiosity of why people do what they do, especially aligning themselves with a school or mascot, even though they themselves did not attend that school or university, led me to the topic of my dissertation. I chose to examine the cultural aspects of high school football in a small town, and all of its connections that provided the glue that, at times, would bond people of a community for a lifetime. What could be gleaned from looking at this phenomenon?

I conducted my study as a single-case study patterned from Dr. Alan Peshkin's study of sports in rural America, and from his book, <u>Growing Up American</u>. It was always my goal to publish my work in book form for anyone who wanted to read it. The following pages are my attempt to do just that. This is also a revised version. A large majority is taken directly from my dissertation. I have provided some additional narrative from my own experiences as an educator and school administrator since the original writing. I hope this work is helpful or interesting for you and serves your purpose.

It is my sole purpose to honor those who live and work in the community and school of Bainesville. I also want to express my sincere thanks and appreciation to those who participated in my research and who were honest and candid with their comments and stories. I worked in the school known here as Bainesville for three years, and it remains an important piece of my life and career.

~ Football Town ~

Chapter One

The Ride into Town

It was Friday night, and there was no moon to be seen. As I drove north on State Road 129, I saw a yellowish glow in the distance; it looked eerie and strange, like a spaceship had landed. I glanced quickly from left to right but saw no other lights. *What could this be*, I asked myself. I drove on, my mind wandering, trying to figure out from where the glow was coming. It was then that I realized that I wasn't sure where I was. I knew that I was headed north on Highway 129 toward a town called

Bainesville, located just twelve miles from the North Carolina border.

The road snaked its way through the mountainous pass and finally rolled sleepily into the town. In front of me was the town square. To the left was a gas station—full service garage and all—and a boutique; to my right was a restaurant and a feed store. Beside the feed store, another road turned off the square, going east toward the yellowish glow. I had determined the origin of the lights; the bright yellowish glow that was now accompanied by the sporadic roar of a crowd was coming from the local high school football field. Without much thought and with hardly any hesitation, I turned right beside the feed store and headed uphill toward the lights, which were now visible along with the poles on which they were mounted.

Paying the three dollar admission at the gate, I found myself almost jogging as I hurried toward the home side of the field. Sounds of whistles, popping pads, and groans came from the direction of the field. The crowd jeered and roared, with individual voices reaching out and beyond the cries of the fans as they stood, eyes locked on a field lined with hash marks and sideline markers. A penalty flag had been thrown against the home team, and it was obvious that the fans did not agree with the referee's call.

I stopped, paused for a moment, and gazed up toward the crowd. *Wow!* I thought. *Where did these people come from?* The stands were packed. There wasn't a seat available anywhere. As I stood next to the fence and watched the game, I got an occasional glance from the gentleman dressed in overalls standing next to me at the fence, stopping from time to time to spit tobacco juice. Students walked past in groups of two or three toward the concession area, laughing and talking among them. I asked the fellow standing next to me how many people the stadium would accommodate. Without looking up, he said, "About three thousand or so."

And then, he turned and walked away. I was amazed. According to my information, there were only 687 students who attended the high school.

I checked into my motel late that night after having dined at the local KFC. I showered and was soon asleep. The next morning, I drove to the high school and introduced myself to the school secretary, who recognized my name from the letter I had mailed and the numerous telephone conversations. The school principal entered the outer office area from a nearby hallway, extended her hand, and said, "Welcome to Bainesville High School, home of the purple and gold."

Chapter Two

Why I Chose Bainesville

Footnote: This is taken directly from my dissertation. The portions in italics represent additional narrative or comments.

In many small and rural communities, the high school serves as a meeting place for the community where town meetings occur, civic events are held, and election posts are located. The school is more than just a place where students attend classes; it is a hub of activity, representing the very fabric of the community. The high school contains all that constitutes the identity of the community: its past, its present, and its future. Rural schools and rural communities are tightly linked and highly interdependent (Versteeg 1993). Bruce Miller (1995, 3), in his study of distressed rural communities, pointed out that "rural schools played a central role in their communities, played a vital part in rural community life and identity formation dating back to the 19th century."

In this study, athletics was used as a lens through which to view the relationship between the community and the high school located in the rural setting. Specifically, the study examined the impact athletics, particularly football, had on the relationship between the community members and the school. As this study unfolded, the idea that athletics and sports—particularly in the deep South—in some strange and mystical way, contained within them an overriding power; and influence was particularly intriguing. Embracing the moments, traditions, and beliefs of the sports culture; transcending themselves beyond the negatives of the past and present; and enabling them to vicariously lavish the hopes and dreams of success in the future seem to be favorite pastimes under the lights of the football stadium. In the book *Friday Night Lights*, H. G. Bissinger (1991) discovered the magic and addiction, the seductive and sometimes brutal power of high school football, as he recounted the story of the small West Texas town of Odessa and their reigning football team. For a town born of dust and deceit, and reborn later through the harshness of the oil booms and busts stretching over four decades, this small Texas town drapes itself with the euphoric experience of Friday night football. Once selected as the town most notable for its stressful lifestyles, high divorce rates, excessive murders, and as one of the poorest towns in all of Texas, its football team has endured. It has been enshrined and has been set high on a pedestal by proclamation from the mayor and city council. Bissinger (1991, 29) described the town as "made for a unique kind of schizophrenia, the highs of the boom years were like a drug-induced euphoria followed by the lows of the bust and the realization that everything you had made during the boom years had just been lost, followed again by euphoria of boom years, followed again by the depression of yet another bust." It's a town of contradictions, filled with men whose grit and character had been baked by the hot West Texas sun and highlighted by a spirit of independence and survival. There were no handouts in Odessa, Bissinger wrote. The topics most reported in the local newspaper, Bissinger noted, were strikes in the oil fields and Permian football, positioned side by side on the front page. The only non-oil related topic appearing on the front page of the *Odessa News*, Berringer wrote, was the "exploits of the Odessa High Yellowjackets" (35–36). In a town where people stood in line for days and hours, without anger to buy their season tickets to Odessa High football, the anticipation of the new season represented a new start and another chance for a state championship under the lights of Friday night. For the people in Odessa, Texas, associating and identifying themselves with the Odessa High Yellowjackets was paramount; and then, in the 1960s when the legacy was transferred to Permian High School Panthers, it "became central to the psyche of the town" (36).

The town of Bainesville, and the county in which the town is located, was born from a boom and bust legacy dating back to the early 1800s when gold was first discovered. Gold diggers, as they were called, poured into town, filling the streets with horses, mules, and wagons and causing a frantic beyond control. The town experienced a sort of chaotic prosperity. But soon, the gold ran short. The shortage, along with the news of the gold strikes in Colorado and California, caused the gold diggers to leave in droves. Bainesville prospered again in the late 1880s when it became a midway stopping point for travelers and traders making their way from the eastern Appalachians southward toward Atlanta and other boomtowns of the early South. As in Odessa, those who remained have a hardened character, great independence, and a strong sense of survival. They have lived through the boom times and the hard times; they find solitude in their churches and reinforce the values and beliefs of the community through their participation in various community events, especially Friday night football. Kevin Horrigan, in his book entitled *The Right Kind of Heroes* (1993), echoed a similar story of hardship, poverty, and dangerous surroundings juxtaposed against the backdrop of a high school football program. For Coach Bob Shannon and his East St. Louis Flyers, those few Friday nights in the fall, preceded by the dog days of August practice, represented a chance for his players to transcend themselves to a higher plane, if only for a brief moment. With every muscle tensed and set to lunge forward, they only thought of inflicting pain and discomfort on the opponent. Getting into a three-point stance, lining up, and waiting for the coach to blow the whistle created a brief moment when Shannon's players had something different to live for, something different to think about—a chance to forget about the drug-infested, dilapidated, deserted, and forgotten neighborhood they called home. Coach Bob Shannon commented that "people here [in East St. Louis] are trapped in a time warp, always talking about when they were in high school; it's a chance to forget about the reality of their surroundings" (44). East St. Louis, or Eastside as it was once called, was once filled with factories and businesses that have long since been abandoned. Boarded-up buildings and vacant lots covered with high weeds and uncut grass lines the streets of East St. Louis. "If the air wasn't so bad, you could climb to the top of the gym at the high school, look west, and see the gleaming Gateway Arch and the skyline of St. Louis, Missouri," lamented Coach Shannon (4). That particular day, as Horrigan described, "some of the team members found a body with bullet holes in the high grass, but this city specializes in bodies with bullet holes. The police were called, and practice went on as scheduled" (4–5). The ritual of football served the same purpose for those in East St. Louis that it served in Odessa, Texas. Football was a ritual act of courage, a means by which a young man's character and manhood were defined, and he was given honor within the boundaries of the community. For the community members in those towns, the ritual of football was transcending.

So what brings people from a community together to watch a football game? Is it merely for the entertainment? Or are there other more significant reasons and motives? Robert Putnam (1995, 70), in his article concerning the decline of America's social capital, noted that "the broader social significance [of coming together in participation of bowling leagues], lies in the social interaction and even occasionally civic conversations over beer and pizza." Like the decline of voting, Putnam retorts, "[the decline of] bowling teams illustrate yet another vanishing form of social capital" (70). From Odessa to East St. Louis or from Mansfield to Bainesville, the ritual of football emerges as a time-honored tradition, where "homecoming parades, school board elections, and school bake sales . . . represent history [that] is carried forward by living people whose tastes and values emerge from this history to influence the present" (Peshkin 1978, 194).

In the rural high school setting of Bainesville, athletics played a major role in the perpetuation and reinforcement of certain values, beliefs, and traditions identified and anointed by the community. Students who participated in school athletics, especially in programs like football and basketball, were given a special status within their school culture and in their community. They had been selected as the representatives of the school. In each game and athletic contest, they (the athletes) did battle with an opponent, a rival. The winning team could claim superiority. The student body, parents, and other community members embraced the celebration. Athletic contests and successful participation in the school's athletic programs became synonymous with overall excellence in achievement and success in life.

This study explored the significance of high school athletic programs—specifically football, the impact of a school's culture on its community, and the level and intensity of community commitment to high school athletics. The study also examined why various community members form bonds of loyalty and allegiance to the local high school. The perceptions of community members and the degree to which they were loyal followers of the local high school and its athletic programs provided the primary framework for this study.

The study of rural communities and rural education, grounded in the literature reviewed, focused on the role of educational reform and/or initiatives, the lack of resources to sustain improvement in the delivery of instruction, and the effects of the lack of business and industry development and its impact on the community from an economic development perspective. Aside from Peshkin's (1978) study of a small rural community, no other research has attempted to uncover the untold stories of the southern rural community and its love and adoration of sporting events, particularly the sport of football. From the stories of the Permian High School Panthers to the Mansfield High Tigers to the East St. Louis High Flyers, the sport of football has been illustrated as the single galvanizing force for the community—extending beyond all boundaries of race, social status, and political affiliation.

An ethnographic approach provided an avenue to uncover the connections between rich traditions embedded within a rural community and the local high school and its athletic programs. An effort was made to determine the relationship between and among high school athletics, school culture, and their effects on a rural community. Emphasis placed primarily on the role of athletics in the development of school culture and the influence of both successful and unsuccessful athletic programs on community involvement in athletic programs was an additional focus. Other questions that helped to frame the initial focus of this study included the following: What effects do time-honored athletic traditions have on a community? What makes the members of a community identify themselves as an extension of the school? How is the loyalty of a community business cultivated to the degree that the business drapes itself with the school's colors and symbols, displays posters and pictures depicting various members of the football or basketball team, and closes early on Friday game days?

Studying the significance of rural high school athletic events as major rallying points for community members provided an avenue for examining the closeness between a school and its community. The researcher, through this study, sought to discover the motivation for closeness and "community spirit" in small rural communities. What roles did school events, such as athletic competitions, play in the development of community support of and loyalty to a high school, such as Bainesville High? Did these roles indicate something deeper and more meaningful than an enthusiasm for sporting events? These questions guided the investigation into the connections between high school athletics and community involvement in and in support of high school athletic programs.

To further illustrate the connection between the high school, its football team, and the community, a recent study of the Bainesville community indicated a high correlation (a score of 4.13 on a 5-point Likert scale) between the school and community in the domain of school sports and extracurricular activities. The study, conducted by the National Study of School Evaluation (NSSE) in 1996, reflected that 91 percent of community members surveyed believed that school-sponsored sports were important features of the school and community. On the same survey, when community members were asked if the school should provide students with multiple opportunities for participation in school sports and school-sponsored extracurricular activities, an overall score of 3.99 resulted. This underscores the perceived importance of high school sports in the small rural community of Bainesville.

So what makes small town athletics special? What makes high school football in small rural communities more special than it is in more urban areas? Attempting to discover the answers to these and related questions was the heart of this study. Prior research on rural communities indicates that a sense of belonging and a sense of family are highly esteemed values for those living in small rural, and sometimes isolated, areas. As one Bainesville High School teacher described it, "In this town (Bainesville), everybody knows everybody else."

Chapter Three

Culture, Symbols, and Traditions: All Strictly Southern

In order to understand the connections between high school athletics and community involvement with the school and how these two elements impact the school culture, a thorough examination of the literature was conducted. The review of literature related to school culture focused on the elements of ritual and ceremony, celebration, traditions, myths, and ethos. Examination of these elements provided evidence of their role in the development of school (organizational) culture.

Literature in rural schools provided a glimpse of the uniqueness of small rural communities and the role that education plays in the community. This literature served as evidence that schools are often centers of their communities and that one of the elements of the school that brings members of a community together is, of course, the athletic programs of the school. In some areas, the predominant sport is football while in other areas, the predominant sport is basketball. In either case, the review of the literature established a framework for connecting the elements of the research topic: the significance of high school athletics, school culture, community development, and school-community connections.

School Culture

The culture of a school is reflected in ceremonies, rituals, celebrations, and symbols, which eventually result in what is commonly referred to as tradition. The significance and culture of school tradition can be seen at football games every Friday night during the fall of the year. It is also evidenced by the overflowing parking lot at the school during awards night or during a chorus program. As Deal and Peterson (1994, 89) explained, "Ceremonies provide a cultural space in which stories are told, rituals enacted, and heroes and heroines are anointed or remembered. During these special events, there is a deeper form of communication that takes place below the surface. Celebrations join past, present, and future. While bonding people to one another and to the important values they share, celebrations provide a functional means for communication. They link myth and structure; so that myth has form and structure comes alive."

Schools demonstrate their culture through ceremonious events, celebrations, and rituals—all of which are symbolic of the school. These events serve as exceptional motivators of students and create a heightened sense of enthusiasm about the school. Sporting events, such as Friday night football games, provide that "cultural space" where all members of the community can come together and become part of a ceremony that links the present with the past and with dreams of the future. Over the years, the ceremonies and celebrations become traditions and are recognized rituals of the school culture.

Symbols

Symbols, like the faces in mirrors, are reflections of the cultures of an organization (Furtwengler and Micich 1991). Symbols take on meaning that is directly connected to the root value of the organization. School symbols such as mascots, lettering, and school colors become almost sacred and acquire immeasurable significance; all those true to the school are expected to honor its symbols. Those who choose to participate in the celebration of athletic contests embrace these symbols as reverent artifacts of the school culture.

Furtwengler and Micich (1991, 14) argued that symbols used to represent school ceremonies provide a "language" that "reflects the school culture." Friday night football games, with crowds roaring and whistles blowing, are symbolic of the high school culture; they represent the past and the future of both adults and students.

At Bainesville High School, situated in the rural foothills of the Blue Ridge Mountains, many symbols represent the indigenous belief that athletics and the activities that surround the games are very much a part of the culture of the community and the culture of the school. For example, a large statue of an Indian, painted purple and gold, stands between the office area and the school's cafeteria. As the school's mascot, the Indian is very symbolic, representing the heritage of both the school and the area. The mountains where Bainesville stands today were once near the center of the great Cherokee Indian Nation. In the early 1830s, most Cherokee were driven from the land. Those who managed to stay did so illegally. Historical documents reflect that some Native American males who were married to white females took the last names of their wives in order to avoid recognition by name by the authorities of the day. The school colors of purple and gold are very symbolic and, again, tie the culture of the school and community together. The gold color designates a link to Bainesville's colorful past as the site of the first gold rush in North America. Even today, the dome on the state's capitol building is plated with gold extracted from the hills near Bainesville many years ago. The purple is a symbolic representation of the courage and spirit of the Native American people who once inhabited the area. At the southeast end of the football stadium stands a large billboard where local businesses pay to display their advertising. At the top of the billboard, a sign reads, Spirit Partners of the Bainesville Indians. Celebrations and rituals such as these help connect the school to its community and assist in transmitting the cultural values of the school from one graduating class to another and one generation to another. These cultural values are further reinforced by the participation of the parents and other community members in celebrations, games, pep rallies, fund-raisers, and other activities.

Ceremonies

Ceremonies are powerful community events that can build a shared identity, spirit, and commitment. They also communicate goals and role-specific expectations and reinforce formal relationships and authority (Deal and Peterson 1994). Values are communicated through symbolic occurrences such as celebrations and ceremonies. It is through this involvement of the community, whose members of the school culture were once, that the values of the identified traditions of a school are passed from one generation to the next. Ceremonies also provide a cultural space in which stories are told, rituals are enacted, and heroes and heroines are anointed (Deal and Peterson 1994, 89). Ceremonies are "episodic occasions" (Deal 1993, 6) "in which the values and heroes are put on display, anointed, and celebrated." For example, during pep rallies at Bainesville High School, the entire student body and all staff stand and sing the school's alma mater. They also have active roles in the cheers and celebratory dances that are planned for pep rallies held in the school's gym. During some pep rallies and at all home games, skits are played out, which demonstrate dominance over the school's opponent. Sometimes, an effigy of the opposing team is "killed" by an Indian spear and then lifted toward the stands, where fans erupt into loud cheers. When the band begins playing the school's fight song, the crowd goes wild again.

Cultural space, referred to by Deal and Peterson, provides a place for members of the school community to come together and reminisce about the past and, perhaps, boast about the present. Whether the cultural space is at the stadium during Friday night rituals in the fall, the school's gymnasium during pep rallies and basketball games, or the school auditorium where those who support the drama program might gather, it is a space where those who are present revel comfortably in their celebration. There they have a sense of belonging. One could view the events that occur within a school, from football and basketball games to dramatic performances to individual performances connected with teaching and learning in classrooms, as a series of ceremonies linked together by tradition and scheduled celebrations. The ritual of ceremony provides the glue that holds together the myths and traditions and the values and beliefs, through time, from one generation to another. The reinforcement of these cultural values and norms occurs through the regularly scheduled ceremonies of the school's various activities.

Rituals

Rituals, according to Deal and Peterson (1994), are routines that have deeper norms and values embedded in them. Rituals that support collaboration, collegiality, and renewal powerfully promote school improvement (88). Deal and Peterson illustrate this point with the story about Dayton's (Ohio) Allen Elementary School, where words of the week were posted on the bulletin board. Every Friday, the entire student body and faculty would gather around the flagpole to watch a skit put on by students to dramatize the meaning of the word or words of the week (88). The practice, in this instance, of promoting and planning instruction and activities around the identification and placing of the word of the week on the bulletin board became ingrained in the norms of the school. It came to be expected. Furthermore, the word-of-the-week skit acted out each Friday became a motivating force for the students.

Events such as football and basketball games, homecoming dances, proms, and pep rallies are all rituals of high school athletics. These events are ritualistic in much the same manner as PTA meetings, school plays, faculty meetings, and school awards banquets in that the norms, values, and mores of the school culture are reinforced. In some instances, some norms, values, and beliefs are modified or changed to reflect the predominant sentiment. Parents and other adults of a community often use various school events to reinforce the perceived value or importance of a particular school culture. For example, parents who make arrangements to watch their sons practice football or their daughters play basketball send a clear message to their children—a message that conveys that participation with the greatest effort is expected. These events convey a perceived importance, reinforce expectations, and, as years go by, progress from mere seasonal rituals to the status of a school tradition.

Chapter Four

All Coaches Will Agree That Games Are Not First
Won on the Field on Friday Nights,
But in the Off-Season

Athletics as Rituals

High school athletics, such as football games or basketball games, are rituals of celebration of the school's finest and greatest. For an athlete, making the team says that he or she has passed the test; his or her endurance and perseverance have been tested, and he or she has met the challenge for the honor of representing the school and its community in competition. High school athletic participation can be considered ritualistic in that it serves as a rite of passage to growth and development as a person. Rituals acquire mythical and symbolic interpretations in the course of time (Driver 1991). As young athletes begin to participate in sports during their seventh and eighth grade years, they begin to hear and believe stories, tales, and myths of playing on the high school team. The high school football coach may have a mystique surrounding him that develops and becomes more embellished as years pass. Stories are told, then retold again and again by the adults in the community—those who played for him and those who, although they did not play, heard the same or similar stories when they were in school.

In *Secular Ritual*, Barbara Myerhoff considered "ritual" to be a kind of rhetoric, calling it a form of "persuasion" and remarking that "rituals are stylized because they must be convincing" (Moore and Myerhoff 1977, 91). In *Reframing Organizations: Artistry, Choice, and Leadership*, Bolman and Deal (1991, 261) pointed out that "all human cultures have used ritual and ceremony to create order, clarity, and predictability, particularly in dealing with issues or problems that are too complex, mysterious, or random to be controlled in any other way." Applied in the context of Friday night high school football games, the ritualistic nature of the games becomes intoxicating. The status of the student and the supporter is often times determined by the degree of participation in the games. "Rituals are always rhetorical and didactic, inducing certain attitudes and convictions, blending wish and actuality until history and accident assume the shape of human intention," (Moore and Myerhoff 1977, 200).

The games, contests, and competitions of the ancient Greek societies, shaped by the mythical beliefs of the citizenry, were ritualistic in nature and created structure for the members of the community to coexist. The symbolic value of competitive sports and games surfaced in other ancient societies, such as that of the Native American Indians. "Sports are extremely rich in symbolization," wrote John

Hargreaves (1986, 12), and "undoubtedly possess the capacity to represent social relationships in a particular, striking way." This is demonstrated by the "pageantry" and "ceremonial celebration" and occurs in conjunction with athletic events and becomes part of the rituals of the community and/or local society.

Athletics in School

High school athletics in a small town or rural community is multidimensional. Both ritualistic and ceremonial, high school athletics represent a means of celebrating the symbolic elements of the community and the school culture. Participation as spectators is a ritual through which the fans "act out the reveries and hopes" of the collected group (Cox 1969, 70), and a form of "social magic" where friends and fans alike become intimate with their dreams of the past or their hopes for their children (Driver 1991). High school athletic competition is the demonstration of a spiritual celebration of the school culture, a mystique of the human spirit and the occasions of triumph and victory.

High school athletic teams are held in high esteem within the school culture. The athletes are set apart from the rest of the student body and are celebrated as the heroes of the school. Players wear special jackets displaying their particular sport and any specific awards they have earned, and on game days, the athletes may dress in similar fashion for the sole purpose of setting themselves apart from the rest. They have special meetings with their coaches, eat together before and after games, and are automatically given certain privileges, such as early released time from school when the team has to travel to an away game. They are celebrated as heroes on game nights as the fans gather, pay entrance fees, and sit collectively on the stands, rooting for the home team. And when the time runs out and the game is over, the people in the crowd rise to their feet, cheering the school's team— whether in victory or defeat.

The rituals of the games bring about a sense of social order. Indeed, Cox (1969, 72, 73) explained that "rituals have a social dimension, and provide a set of connections through which emotions can be expressed"; and thus, they become "social fantasies." High school athletic events, therefore, are mechanisms through which the various members of the community come together for a common purpose. Through participation in the event—as a parent, a player, or a fan—a common bond is formed and is continuously reinforced throughout the athletic season.

The connections among the rural school, its athletic programs, and the rural community run very deep. In *School-Community Relations Under Reform*, Crowson (1992, 23), in his discussion of schools and their communities, wrote that "a continuity between home and school, and a blending of school as a focus for people's lives outside the home are common themes in examinations of nineteenth-century schools." Crowson pointed out that in the nineteenth century and early twentieth century, "the schoolhouse was controlled by its community and especially by its parents" (24). Many nineteenth-century schools, Crowson (1992) wrote, were characterized by broad parental participation and reflected closely the needs and interests of their communities.

The findings discovered by Crowson clearly illustrate the fact that parents and other pertinent constituents had significant impact on the direction and development of the schools. As Crowson stated, parental participation reflected the needs and interests of the school's community; thus, bonds of connectedness were created through their participation and their influence in establishing the direction and priorities for the school's development as an institution. High school athletics, especially football, lends itself as a major connector between the school and the community—thus, providing parents and other interested community members a sense of ownership, stewardship, and a sense of belonging.

This sense of belonging takes on the value as family whenever the child of a parent participant is a member of the high school football team. The very fact that the child, the student athlete, holds such status as a team member gives the parents informal power, authority, and status in the community.

In *Growing Up American*, Peshkin (1978) described in rich detail the local control of schooling . . . in the community of Mansfield. From an overflow crowd at the Friday night football game to inserting a liberal dose of religion into the school's curriculum to selecting an incoming superintendent of schools who was suitably "country," the community of Mansfield remained fully in possession of its schools and vice versa (Crowson 1992).

High school athletic events serve many purposes. For the student athlete, they provide a way for the student to excel and achieve on the field, which can have an impact on his/her classroom performance. Secondly, they provide an avenue for other students, those who are not athletes, to participate as fans and loyal supporters in an activity that highlights their school, thus facilitating a bond between the students and their school. School pride and allegiance develop as a result. High school athletics also provide a megaphone through which the members of the community (students, alumni, teachers, and other supporters) can cheer and celebrate the school's triumphs in Friday night battles. High school athletics can evoke a sense of belonging and purpose within the school and can lead to the development or enhancement of loyalty, allegiance, and school pride.

Athletics in the Community

For the parents and other members of the community, athletic events—and in this case, high school athletic events—serve as a conduit for reliving past dreams and aspirations. Friday night football games or Tuesday night basketball games provide for spectators the opportunity to reenact what could have been: the touchdown they could have scored, the winning basket at the buzzer during the championship game, the final heroic act that would have endured for all time. Indeed, the Friday night football games and midweek basketball games become institutional events where parents and other community members meet to reminisce about the past and to "act out" their fantasies and dreams of athletic triumph (Cox 1969).

For community members who are supporters of the games—and the school—participation as a spectator plays a significant role. It is their way of connecting with the school and its culture. In some respects, it is their way of staying young and re-experiencing their youth. These participants, whose sons and daughters may or may not have ever played a competitive sport, choose to actively support the teams and attend the games. They arrive at the stadium or gym dressed ceremoniously in the school's colors, displaying Go, Fight, Win! on the windows of their vehicles. They completely embrace the identity of the school and its traditions, which are symbolic of their values and beliefs. Rain, sleet, nor cold dreary weather will keep these fans away. They drive forty or fifty miles without hesitation to attend games and show their support. Attendance at the games becomes a ritual in itself, with the formation of smaller social groups who maintain communication and affiliation with one another.

Stories, Fairy Tales, and Myths

Organizational stories, according to Gordon (1992), are stories that people in organizations tell to recount incidents from an oral history of the organization's past. The central characters are members of the organization. Such stories provide a "cognitive repertoire of scripts fitting a host of organizational settings" (7–8). The heartbeat of an organization can often be judged by the stories that are told and retold about past events and former characters (members) of the organization. Such storytelling by those anchored members of the organization is a subtle yet powerful illustration of how deeply the values of the organization are embedded.

Myths and fairy tales, on the other hand, are used to convey and transmit a certain persona. Myths, Bolman and Deal (1991, 256) wrote, "Support claims of distinction and transform a mere organization into a beloved institution." An example of the perpetuation of the values and traditions of schools would be the telling and retelling of stories about the past. For example, a father recounting to his high school–aged son the details of a touchdown run during the homecoming game in 1960 or the tales of a once-famous band that played at all of the proms and after-the-game dances would illustrate the high level of importance placed on the continuation of stories. Reshaped with grandier details and descriptions, these stories serve to reinforce the importance of participating in high school athletics and clarify the expectation for the future success of individual athletes. They further reinforce the community's expectations for establishing a social order.

In rural communities, schools often serve as meeting places for other events. The local high school in many instances is the hub for many of the activities that occur in the rural community. To fully understand the underlying expectations and norms related to the role of the school in a rural community, one must first gain an awareness of community in rural areas.

Chapter Five

Historical Significance of Competitive Games

Fully understanding the role of high school athletics in a small town or rural community, places where the activities of little league baseball to high school football are interconnected, the historical significance of competitive games in societies must be examined. Evidence of competitive sports can be found in most societies, and despite the claim of rare and isolated primitive tribes who had no competitive games, sports can be counted among the few cultural universals of mankind (Luschen and Sage 1981). The role and existence of competitive sports (recreation) as a major factor of influence can be found in numerous ancient societies—from the Minoan culture of Crete in the third and second millennium BC, the city-state of Greece in the sixth, fifth, and fourth centuries BC; the urban societies of the Roman Empire from the first century AD until the end of the fourth century when the termination of the Olympic Games marked the end of a sporting era (25).

The presence and prominence of athletic contests in the lifestyles of the Greeks and Romans are evidenced by numerous references in *The Iliad* (28). Some athletic events, many that remain part of the modern Olympic Games, have their origin in ancient Greece. The throwing of the javelin, the discus, archery contests, boxing, and the footrace are all related either specifically or in part to the competitions practiced in the ancient Olympic Games. In *Sport, Culture, and Personality,* D. Calhoun (1987, 78) found that Homer, in the early days of Greece, "memorialized the urge to always be the best and to excel [over] others." The influence of Homer marked the beginning of an era in which the power and influence of the games drive the behavior of society. This "memorialized games" of competitive athletic events reinforced formally the status, role, and traditions that had evolved from competitions much like the cockfights in Bali (Cox 1969), where local policemen in effect ignored the various cockfights, which were illegal. The cockfights had become an embedded tradition and ritual for the male-dominated society. The cockfights provided a social structure in a society immersed in poverty and lacking the economic infrastructure to facilitate other means of establishing social strata.

In ancient societies, athletic contests were "constrained by a code of conduct accepted and well understood by heroes—the athletes" (29). Contests in armor were never brought to an end by bloodshed and death; rather, the contest was one of courage, bravery, and nerves—often carried out by those who had recently returned from battles for the ruling party.   Similarly, the wrestling match between Aias and Odysseus was stopped by Achilles with the words: "No longer press each other, nor were you out in pain.   Victory is with both; take equal prizes and depart," (Homer, *The Iliad*, Book 23: 735, 29). This act of limiting or restricting the extent of the athlete by Achilles is an example of how the ancient games played a pivotal role in shaping the cultural values of the ancient societies.   The demeanor of the athletes who won the contests was as important as the victory itself:

> "Do thou, father of Zues, that ruleth over the height of Atabyrium, grant honour to the hymn ordained in praise of any Olympic victorand to the hero who hath found fame for his prowess as a boxer; and do thou give him grace and reverence in the eyes of citizens and strangers, too.   For he goeth in a straight path that hateth insolence," quoted from Pindar, O. O., Book 7: 84–95. (Luschen and Sage 1981, 36)

The games, contests, and competitions of the ancient Greek societies created structure for the members of the community to coexist, which was shaped by the mythical beliefs of the citizenry. The Native American Indians revered the symbolic value of competitive sports and games, and this symbolic value surfaces in other ancient societies. "Sports are extremely rich in symbolism," writes John Hargreaves (1986, 12), and "undoubtedly possess the capacity to represent social relationships in a particular, striking way." This is demonstrated by the "pageantry" and "ceremonial celebration" that occurs in conjunction with athletic events.

The games played by Native Americans were an integral part of their culture (Luschen and Sage 1981). With the native people, there were many myths that emerged. Several games were viewed as being sanctioned by the gods and cultural heroes of their people. Many games were used by Native Americans to settle disputes. In the late 1830s, the Cherokee and Choctaw tribes in Georgia and other parts of the southeastern United States played a stickball game to settle stakes of each tribe's land (54).

Additionally, the American team sport games of football, basketball, baseball, and softball have their origins in Native American cultures. The importance of the games in the lives of the North American Indians was reinforced by the belief that their gods played and approved of the games (73). Games in the ancient Indian cultures facilitated cohesion within the tribal communities and provided a means for the members of the tribe to reinforce the norms of their culture. The cultural rituals of games in Native American Indian society had a direct impact on the behavior of tribal members. Ritual and ceremony were very much a part of their social structure.

Fast forward to 2011; ritual and ceremony are still very much a part of the ethos and traditions that define societies and communities around and throughout the world. We still celebrate the World

Olympic Games every four years, and great importance and significance is placed on the awarding and selection of the city and country who will serve as the international host for the games.

Indeed, from the small pee wee league football game on a cool brisk Saturday morning to the Friday night high school football game under the lights of the local stadium, to the gymnasium or arena where athletes compete on an international level, the same enthusiasm can be summoned by those who fill the seats of the stadium or arena or lawn chairs in the grass on the sideline of an old cow pasture turned football field. The ghosts and unknown legends of the past, some ancient in time, render their power of adrenalin and revelry that transforms the ordinary into extraordinary.

The enthusiasm is contagious and timeless, and provides a unity and identity beyond description. The Greeks and Romans did it; the ancient European and Napoleonic people did it; the tribesmen of the new colonies did it; the native and indigenous people from various continents did it, and it remains today a viable and significant part of the tapestry of human interaction and connection.

Chapter Six

Athletics, Sports, and Games

Friday night football games: The sound of shoulder pads clapping together, the coolness of a fall night, and steam rising from the players as they return to the sidelines—all represent a ritual and tradition that is embedded in the American culture. High school athletic events, in effect, serve many masters. For the student athletes, it provides a way for the student to excel outside the classroom. It also teaches self-discipline, teamwork, and the desire to persevere.

Many coaches argue that the participation in competitive sports has a positive effect on the student's motivation and performance in academics. The reasons cited are often related to discipline, character, boundaries, and hard work. Excelling in sports, many coaches proclaim, provides the student athlete with an overwhelming amount of self-confidence which builds strength and persistence in other areas of life where perhaps optimum performance is more challenging.

For parents and other community members, athletic events—those dealing particularly with high school or college sports—act as conduits for reliving past dreams. Friday night football games or Tuesday night basketball games or whatever the major sport of the school might be affords the opportunity for parents and fans alike to reenact in their minds what could have been: the touchdown they could have scored, the interception on the five yard line, or the winning basket at the buzzer in the championship game—the final heroic act that would endure all time.

And, yet, competitive sports serve as a rite of passage for girls and boys, young men and young women athletes all over the world. I think, however, that it has become a uniquely American iconic phenomenon in that the active participation in a competitive sport provides a way in which the values of a work ethic, expectations, positive perspectives, and perseverance through hard and tough times, are all conveyed and communicated to the youngsters and young people. It's very much a part of the American way of life. It is part of the American tapestry of what is seen and thought of as the American Character. Athletes don't need a face for an identity, just mud, blood, and the modern version of war paint. The act of participating as a member of a competitive team with a fan base, if only the few parents of the kids who play, is noteworthy enough to last a lifetime.

There are few things truly iconic and significant in the American scene and landscape: Sunday church, summer weddings, family reunions, birthdays, high school graduations, and Friday night football. Bainesville, in many ways, represents a slice of the American pie, an "Americana" people try desperately to hold onto and cherish with every fiber of their being. It is true what Alan Peshkin said in his study of Manchester in his book, <u>Growing up American</u>, "It's a way of life connected to the lifeblood of the community." Just ask any person you see dressed in the colors of their school with painted faces, adorned color-coordinated clothing, chairs, cars, and campers. It's contagious enthusiasm at its best.

Chapter Seven

Things Are Different in the Country

Rural Communities and Schools

In rural areas, school and community values and norms are aligned and serve as markers on the horizon, like needles on a compass that guide the establishment of values and beliefs and transfer traditions from one generation to the next. In examining Amish communities, Miller (1992, 16) found that the community and school provided a "seamless continuum of values and norms." Essentially, all of the members of the Amish community held similar values and beliefs, which were reinforced through both their teachings in school and church, as well as through the interactions of the adults of the community. Miller's study of an Amish community supports the idea that a close-knit community is a functional community that certain specific norms, values, beliefs, and traditions become embedded in the culture. Coleman describes a functional community as a consistent social structure, linked by family and school, which forms an "extended network of kinship, friendship, and work relations that pervade the community" (Coleman 1987, 147). For example, in small rural communities, according to Miller (1992, 17), when a child begins experiencing difficulties (in school or with some other community activity), a member of the social network would most likely "communicate to the parents and provide support for the child," which illustrates the connectedness of the community.

In rural areas, schools and their communities share a deep sense of connectedness and reliance on each other for the establishment and reinforcement of the norms and values of both the school and the community. The sense of a shared mission and a mutual support between the rural school and the rural community was illustrated in the study of the Caswell County Training School (Siddle-Walker 1993). In this study, the members of the community were found to exhibit "self-reliance, sacrifice, and a sense of community responsibility . . . for the school" (163). Siddle Walker found that "parents' belief that the school cared about the success of their children might [have] helped explain the 'respect' and 'trust' that parents had . . . towards the community schools and their support of them" (172). The author notes that parents and the school had a "collective stake in the educational process of the youth in the community" (173). Siddle Walker's study demonstrates that "the interaction between the school and community" was a "collaborative relationship, a kind of mutual ownership in which the community and school looked out for each others' needs—the parents depended on the school's expertise, guidance, and academic vision. They were united in a common mission to provide a quality education for their children," (175).

Alan Peshkin builds on these themes in his study of change in rural education (1978) at Mansfield High School. He found that at the heart of a rural community's resistance to change is the sense of a rural community's desire to protect their "school-community accord" and that a sense of "intimacy, belonging, and nurturance" exists between the rural community and the school. Peshkin describes Mansfield High School, the site of his ethnographic study on the role of the high school in a rural community, as a "whirlwind of activity" (147). As Peshkin points out, the school is "Like a circus boasting 'Come one! Come all; Fun for the entire family'" (147). Peshkin further explained that the community members viewed the schools "as irreplaceable and priceless, the marks of an unchanging order" (207).

These findings illustrate connections that may exist between a rural school and its community. The teaching that occurs within a small rural school is a reflection of its community and the values and traditions that the members of the community deem most significant. This teaching is defended and passed from generation to generation. The resistance to change, as noted by Peshkin in his study of the Mansfield community, is directly related to maintaining what is known and recognized by the members of the community. Outdated vocational programs, for example, may be embedded in the thoughts and minds of community members as being viable and having purpose when in actuality; the programs do not prepare students for postsecondary work.

In *Growing Up American*, Peshkin (1978, 133) remarked, as he describes "pep and spirit," that "a display of spirit is desirable, and concern about its expression and magnitude is a recurring issue." He stresses that pep and spirit are maintained through their role in the school culture and are evidenced by established rituals. High school athletics is a ritual from which stories are created, heroes and heroines are anointed, and the culture of the school is solidified. The high school football field or gymnasium, therefore, provides an atmosphere where school spirit can be nurtured and energized; thus, the ritual of the games becomes multidimensional. In rural settings, the rituals of these games involve the entire community and take on an added significance, becoming expectations as well. The level of involvement from community members is often parallel to their status within their community. This phenomenon is similar to the parallelism that exists between the status and participation in church or religious activities within a rural community. Peshkin found that most activities that occurred within the Mansfield community were intimately linked to the school.

In Mansfield, as Peshkin (1978) pointed out, the schools in large measure serve the community. Small schools typically serve a community nucleus and "invite strong support from parents and community members as well as a closer working relationship among the school staff" (Peshkin 1978, 2). These findings are indicative of the perceived importance and embedded value of loyalty and allegiance to one's community. This theme is illustrated throughout Peshkin's study of Mansfield where the importance of the high school serving as the "hub of activity" and "the place where when lights are out in other public settings, save for the Laundromat and the taverns, there is likely something happening" (147).

School and Community

It can be assumed that the relationship between school and community involves an array of interactions between members of a community and members of a school. The aspect of community, in this description, suggests a specific geographic region, area, or neighborhood—with the school being a part of the larger community. In order to understand the concept of community relations in context with the school, the idea of community must be fleshed out and thoroughly examined. Merz and Furman (1997) suggested a perspective that assigns an analytical continuum between Tonnies's (1887/1957) gemeinschaft, "natural will," and gesellschaft, "choices made on the basis of rational will," as a way of viewing the development of community bonds. Applying the concept of gemeinschaft to the examination of community, as Merz and Furman pointed out, it can be said that people did not choose a community—they were born into it. They were generally not free to choose their religion, where they lived, or their circle of friends (18). In gesellschaft, Merz and Furman (1997, 18) contended, "Solutions can be negotiated to assure that they are advantageous to both parties." Redfield (1941/1950), after studying several different cultures developed the theory that gemeinschaft and gesellschaft qualities could coexist in cultures, noting that the "folkways" defined the culture of villages and communities. In the early part of the twentieth century during the Industrial Revolution period, people moved from the farms and rural areas to urban areas near cities where industrial development had occurred. The sense of community, therefore, experienced a drastic change.

The idea of community as a cohesive collection of people noted by Tocqueville (1835/1945), as referenced by Merz and Furman (1997, 24), suggested that "Americans balanced individualism and society through family life, religious beliefs, and a unique tendency to form volunteer civic groups." Robert Bellah in *Habits of the Heart* (1985, 250) explored the struggle between individualism and commitment to others and noted that "people developed loyalty to others in the context of families, small communities, religious congregations and life-style enclaves." Bellah (1985) offered a different definition of "community." He spoke of "real communities" as "communities of memory constituted by their past" (153). Bellah further noted that the telling of stories of a community reinforced the meaning of existence within the community, giving the members of the community a sense of belonging and a sense of connection. Etzioni (1993, 160) referred to community as a vehicle, noting that "people sign on to a manifesto of principles regarding responsibility to others." From this perspective, the concept of community becomes utilitarian, used as a vehicle to reflect the progress of a structured organization of people. It mirrors a contractual agreement between the members of a community and a set of ideals or principles formally or informally devised within the community. In contrast, most churches are closer to gemeinschaft in that they serve as a "gathered community" for individuals who voluntarily associate with one another because of shared spiritual values.

Another view of community was noted by Merz and Furman (1997) from Friedman (1982), who imposed the view that people were involved simultaneously in a number of communities and suggested a model for "community of choice" (148) as a means of clarifying the concept of community. Defining school-community relations or connections, then, becomes difficult and somewhat confusing task. Sergiovani (1994) pointed out that "the loss of community" was the heart of the problem for educational reform. While others, such as Crowson and Boyd (1993), argued that "community-connections experiments" such as site-based management and parent-involvement programs "attempts to strengthen the links between schools and local communities."

Writers like Ernest Boyer (1995, 15) have concluded that "community is without question the glue that holds an effective school together." The arguments presented by Boyd, Crowson, and Boyer parallel the assertions of Schmuck (1992, 5) in her study of the advantages of small schools and small communities as she noted, "there is an intimate connection between the schools and community [in small towns], and there exist an unusual commitment to place and the idea of belonging." Schmuck pointed out that the concept of "communitarianism," inspired by Amitai Etzioni and written about in the book *The Good Society* by Bellah et al. (1991, 5), as a "movement to connect people to their communities and to each other." This, Schmuck ascertained, was what came naturally to small rural towns and communities and their schools but was somewhat more difficult to achieve in urban and suburban centers where schools competed with other institutions for resources.

Determining the role community plays in the bigger picture of school-community relations, according to Crowson (1992), involves a broadly defined construct, with many variations of interpretations. To some educators, the term "community-relations" and "public relations" are synonymous (Crowson 1992, 9). John Goodlad (1984), in his book entitled *A Place Called School*, described the idea of school-community relations as "performing common educational functions . . . using shared resources" (351–352). "Community" is described by Galbraith (1992, 37) as "the social space in which people perceive common problems . . . the extent to which members organize themselves to effectively confront these problems." Crowson concluded that at least two interpretations of community relations in context with schools existed and required close study. One interpretation of school-community relations conveyed a central purpose connected with the maintenance of community support for the schools, thus requiring great amounts of time and energy for establishing and maintaining relationships between people and groups whose goal or vision met with overlapping commonality and concern for effective educational processes.

The second interpretation discussed by Crowson explained that community relations were inherently connected with direct parent participation in the process of schooling, being involved through parent organizations, volunteer efforts, and para-professionalism.

Still, another impression of the construct of school-community relations is revealed by Beck and Murphy (1996, 85) in their review of what they call "the community imperative," in which the works of several authors were discussed. Authors (Bryk and Driscoll 1988, 3) suggested that "the community plays an important role in promoting satisfaction, engagement, and learning" (Beck and Murphy 1996, 85). They point out that "adult commitment" has "important social and academic benefits . . . to students" (Bryk et al. 1993, 287). In *Growing Up American*, Alan Peshkin (1978) described in rich detail the local control of schooling in the small Midwestern agricultural community of Mansfield. Although, Crowson (1992, 27) pointed out that

"Mansfield-type" relationships between school and community can still be found, even in city neighborhoods, James Coleman (1985/1987), as Crowson contends, argued that "the close-knit, functional communities exemplified by Mansfield were a vanishing breed" (Crowson 1978, 27).

In contrast, Jonathan Kozol (1992) described with vivid detail the atrocities of the children who lived and attended school in the various urban communities included in his study on the inequalities in schools. One must conclude that urban area schools and communities are different from rural schools and communities; perhaps the rural culture is not as harsh. In an interview with Kozol, the school counselor of PS 79, as he (1992, 105) described it, the school counselor made this observation about the students who attended the school: "It's quite remarkable how much these children see. You wouldn't know it from their academic work. Most of them write poorly. There is a tremendous gulf between their skills and capabilities. I mean, it says so much about the squandering of human worth."

In summary, it is pertinent to point out that a significant relationship exists between the community in general and the high school in a rural setting. Viewing the relationship between the community and high school's predominant athletic programs within the context of a rural setting provided a unique perspective that stretched beyond the aspects of entertainment and belonging.

The community's involvement, connectedness with the school, and the impact on school culture of the interplay between these elements creates an extremely complex and ambiguous social paradigm. The confines of a rural community provided a unique backdrop from which to analyze the social interplay and significance of community. The relationship between rural schools and their communities was evident in the literature but lacked a specific study that examined sports as the viewing lens. The study of Bainesville, perhaps, has provided the viewing lens.

Chapter Eight

Football and the Bainesville Community: Tradition Abounds

The review of the literature related to rural schools and rural communities revealed a deep affectionate interaction between the local high school in general and the community's dependence on the activities the school provides. After reviewing the literature, the connectedness between school and community that Alan Peshkin wrote about in his book *Growing Up American* is much more readily understood. The high school in Bainesville is truly the heart of the community. The following account illustrates how the school is both a reflection of the community and a product of the community, with athletics playing a major role in shaping the values and traditions of both the school culture and the community culture. This chapter, in presenting the story of Bainesville, clarifies the importance of tradition, symbolism, ceremony, and celebration and examines the ways in which the community of Bainesville embraces the high school and its football teams and the ways in which the community maintains its culture.

The football program provides an avenue through which the individual community member can take on active and authoritative roles, gaining social status in the community and becoming highly visible among their peers. These roles may include announcing the home games on Friday nights, selling hot dogs in the concession stand or tickets at the gate, or serving as president of the Bainesville Athletics Booster Club. One former student and football player described the Friday night home football game as the "main attraction in town; the place you want to be if you live in this community."

This chapter discusses further the implications of the interview and archival data in that the local high school plays an integral role in vitality of the Bainesville community. The high school's football program has also played a primary role in shaping the values and traditions of both the school and the community. The political strife attached to the high school's football program is aptly illustrated in the two coaching crises described in this chapter and provided support for the argument that the values and traditions connected with how the concept of "community" was defined and demonstrated through the levels of concern, anxiety, and enthusiasm exhibited by members of the Bainesville High School fans. Bainesville is, indeed, a small rural mountain town whose community ethos and mores are steeped in the tradition of the way life has been and in the history of Friday night football.

Steeped in Tradition and History

The community of Bainesville is steeped in tradition and history, holding to the past as motivation for the present. The high school is located only two miles from the point where the original gold strike occurred over one hundred years ago, which at the time thrust Bainesville into an orbit of prosperity and egocentric thinking. Controversies and conflict over industrial development near old mining sites still ignite hostility and resentment from some in the community. Since Bainesville is located in what was once the heart of the Cherokee nation, many of the community members celebrate the teachings of the Cherokee people. Gatherings were held monthly on property that has been designated as a sacred, ceremonial area. Symbols of Bainesville High School—like the Indian, the totem pole, and the rock—reflect the community's values and tradition that seem connected to the area's past.

The Bainesville Indians were named for the indigenous Native American people who once inhabited the area and were part of the Cherokee Indian Nation; hence, the Bainesville High School mascot is the Indian. He has no specific name but is simply referred to as the Indian. A statue of the Indian standing ten feet tall guards the school cafeteria, one hand positioned above his eyes as if to shade his vision from the sun and the other hand holding a shield to his rib cage. He gazes across the cafeteria and out toward the mountains in the distance.

The Indian and the ties to the Indian culture represent a major aspect of the school culture. Like the Cherokees, a persistent struggle to survive can be measured in the competitive spirit of the students at Bainesville High School. This pride is exhibited in numerous subtle ways. Students never mark or deface the Indian, although graffiti can be found in many other places on campus. Although students are frequently involved in pranks and games, they will not write on the Indian. During breaks in the school day, students pile their book bags around the base—the feet—of the Indian, appearing to pay tribute and respect to the school's mascot and major symbol. Day after day, this was observed; it seemed to be a ritual of reverence. I was continually amazed that no book bags were stolen or tampered with as they lay at the Indian's feet. The Indian represents a significant and respected symbol of the school.

At graduation time, it has been a long-standing tradition for a select group of seniors to break into the school, kidnap the Indian, and to take him to wherever the high school graduation ceremony was being held. Graduation in May 1996 was no exception. The graduation ceremony was held in the gymnasium of a college located to the south of town, and the Indian was there. He was positioned so that every member of the senior class could touch his arm or his shield as they began their procession into the arena, preparing to end one journey and begin another. As one teacher explained, "This ritual has been carried out for over thirty years. It is one that is accepted, even expected, by the administration and the parents." At the May 1996 ceremony, as I watched from the stage, every senior paused beside the Indian; some gave a serious glance, some wiped tears, and some broadcasted smiles. They touched his massive arm or his shield and then walked in cadence to their places and were seated in unison. It was a powerful and moving ritual, carried out in silence and with respect.

The Indian (as symbol of the school) and the graduation ceremony are remarkably interwoven and illustrate the rural culture's connectedness with the experience of high school. The traditions of both the community and the school come together at graduation. In *From Beginning to End: The Rituals of Our Lives*, Robert Fulghum (1995, 52) remarked: "Rituals do not always involve words, occasions, officials, or an audience. Rituals are often silent, solitary, and self-contained. The most powerful rites of passage are reflective—when you look back on your life again and again, paying attention to the rivers you have crossed and the gates you have opened and walked on through, the thresholds you have passed over. I see ritual when people sit together silently by an open fire, remembering."

The Indian, for these students, provided a prompt to pause and to be reflective to remember the past as they go forth to face their future.

Just outside the high school gymnasium stands a twenty-foot Indian totem pole. In the Indian culture, totem poles symbolize social and religious structure and are usually placed just outside the dwelling. Totem poles symbolically identify the tribe and their beliefs.

The totem pole outside the Bainesville High School gymnasium began as a project for a specific group of students, identified by one of the high school teachers as a group that was planning to drop out of school. They had become disinterested and had disassociated themselves from the other students. They had lost or never developed a sense of "school spirit." The teacher asked permission to oversee a special project—constructing a totem pole—with these students, a project aimed at keeping them in school and rekindling their interest in being there. Permission was granted by the school principal, and work soon began on the totem pole. The teacher recruited a member of the community who specialized in carving totem poles to serve as an advisor and took the students to the library to research the origins of totem poles, specifically those of the Cherokee. Once the research was completed, the students and their teacher set out to design and build the totem pole. Many long hours of labor went into the project. Adam Boatwright, the teacher in charge of the totem pole project, shared the story of the students who suddenly found a purpose—a sense of connection with the school. He recalled that the students were reluctant at first but found ownership once they were involved with the project: "They resisted at first, but then, they began to get excited about it. I think that it was because they could see something coming from their efforts. In the end, you couldn't drag those boys from working on that thing. In fact, the day we were digging the holes for the footing for the totem pole, it began to rain. I want you to know that those boys stood right out there in that rain and kept working. I had to make 'em stop." (Adam Boatwright, teacher)

Today, the totem pole stands as a beautifully painted symbol of the school and the kids who labored to complete it. The totem pole project was successful in that the students who worked on it remained in school for the completion of that school year. They found a school connection in which they could feel ownership and pride.

The only marquee to announce or inform the community about school current events is "the rock." The rock is a symbol of school pride and was put into place only a few years ago, in 1992. The huge rock is located at the south end of the school campus and is used by the students, mainly cheerleaders, to display slogans for sports teams and to announce important events. "It's a way of letting the community knows what is going on," one student explained. Use of the rock is managed by student groups but mostly by the cheerleaders and sports teams of the school. The rock is never abused or misused. Unwritten protocol exists as to the management of the rock and is passed orally from class to class.

The rock is given a prominent place in the BHS yearbook. Students are photographed standing around the rock and sitting on it. It is a revered place and a symbol of the school. The rock and the way in which it is managed represent another element in the verbal and symbolic history of the Bainesville High School students and their school. The rock serves notice to the community. As one member of a student group described the rock: "It's like a spirit board, I guess you could say. But during football and basketball, it's the cheerleaders' job to keep it painted, and we keep the community informed about what's going on."

Heart of the Community

The school is also the heart of the community in that many of the community's celebrations and ceremonies are connected to the school. Bainesville High School serves as a base for social interaction, hosting many social-community events—from football games, school dances, car shows, dramatic productions, and parent meetings to bonfires and pep rallies. The school's festivities and celebrations have become expectations of the community. Some of these activities are simple and require only a few people to organize while others are more complex, requiring many hours of planning and the combined efforts of numerous people. From the pep rally for the seniors and the homecoming game to the bonfire and homecoming week festivities, the community embraces the celebrations of the school and acknowledges their importance in the community. The school events of homecoming week are embedded into conversations all over town. The expectation that community members participate in the school's celebrations and activities is always present; however, community members determine their own levels of participation. To do otherwise would provoke an immediate response from those in the community who feel their way of doing things is being threatened. One teacher expressed that the activities during homecoming week were hectic and exhaustive but were strongly supported by the community. During a planning meeting for the homecoming week festivities in October 1996, it was suggested that the selection of a homecoming king be eliminated from the proposed list of events. An angry response from the community occurred almost immediately. Telephone calls were made to the high school principal and the superintendent. Parents called teachers expressing their concerns about the change in the ceremony. The selection of the homecoming king had been a tradition at the school since the beginning of the football program itself and, apparently, was expected in the community. It was unthinkable to suggest that the event be eliminated. The cheerleaders, with the support of their parents, filed their complaint about the possible elimination of the event. Letters of protest from the student body were also received. The principal quickly called for a meeting of the planning committee where the issue was thoroughly discussed once again, with the final decision being not to change any of the events that had occurred in past years. The homecoming king would be announced and crowned at the homecoming dance held on Saturday night, following the homecoming football game on Friday.

The notion that the community lives to celebrate is strongly evident in the ways the people of the community freely express their opinions about the football team. Year after year when the autumn winds begin to swirl, the fans return to the high school's football stadium to watch the Friday night games. Like old warriors who gather for a war dance, the people of the community, both young and old, gather to see the latest edition of the Bainesville football team do battle with the enemy. They jump to their feet when the "favorite son" of the year, usually a running back, breaks open for a large gain. They rise up in anger when they feel the team has been unfairly accused of an infraction by an official. They celebrate the wins, both large and small, and show anguish when the team loses. They reaffirm their connection and sense of purpose through their participation in and attendance at the games and other events associated with the high school's football program. For sixty minutes on each Friday night during the months of September, October, and November, the community and the school are one. The last game of the season not only closes another chapter of Bainesville football history, it serves as a night of honor for family and community as the parents and family members of each player are recognized during halftime.

Homecoming week is filled with traditions and celebrations, culminating on the playing field at the homecoming football game. At halftime, the crowning of the homecoming queen occurs and the homecoming king is introduced over the public address system. The queen and her court are driven in majestic style around the outer perimeter of the football field as all who are present stand and cheer. Other homecoming week festivities include spirit contests; a parade that features floats designed and constructed by various groups, classes, or clubs within the school; and a midweek bonfire.

The bonfire is a ritual that occurs at many high schools and is usually held on a night during the week preceding the homecoming game. The mood at Bainesville High School during homecoming week in November 1997 was jubilant. The collection of wood and other materials to be consumed by the bonfire had been the topic of conversation for days.

It was also a topic on the agenda of the weekly administrative meeting of the high school staff: Who would supervise the stacking of the wood? Who would orchestrate the lighting and burning of the wood? Who would be in charge of the sound system and the music at the bonfire? A lot of emphasis was placed on the bonfire, and a great deal of energy was expended on planning it. It was a major event. In his book *The Feast of Fools*, Harvey Cox (1969, 23, 24) explained, "A festival embraces the moment. It is tied to no other goals. Celebration links us to both the past and the future . . . and may include something that is still only hoped for."

The bonfire and all that is associated with it may be viewed as a ritual that marks the time and date of a significant event. "Ritualization involves both improvisation and the establishment of repeatable form," (Driver 1991, 30). The bonfire provides an outlet through which students; athletes, parents, teachers, and other community members can express themselves, either by their parents present at the event or by their active participation in planning for it.

The night of the Bainesville High School bonfire was indeed a memorable event. Students, players, and parents gathered as the blaze from the fire reached with its fiery fingers toward the night sky. Standing on the south side of the fire, looking toward the front of the gym, the silhouette of the totem pole could be seen against the orange sky. The teachers and administrators, as well as some of the parents, stood in the background shaking rock-filled, gold milk jugs that were trimmed in bright purple. Sayings like "Go Indians!," and, "Go, Fight, Win!;" were inscribed on the golden jugs in purple lettering. Students danced and cheered to music that was blaring from speakers mounted on the tailgates of two Chevy trucks. These were students' trucks, one a late model and the other an older model Chevy that had been newly painted a few days before. The dry pine logs that had been stacked for days created an inferno, roaring almost in cadence with the music.

The homecoming parade is a big event. The parade is held at exactly 1:45 p.m. on Friday afternoon of game day. As local sheriff's officers barricade the streets, the parade proceeds through the parking lot of the school, past the middle school, down Main Street and around the town square to the college, then around the square again, and back through the gates of the school. I observed this event from the last float in the parade, the fifteenth one. There were beautifully decorated floats representing the Automotive Club, Beta Club, student council, football team, cheerleaders, and numerous other groups. The Automotive Club displayed a freshly painted car engine on their float. Ribbons, balloons, and streamers of purple and gold adorned the engine, with slogans that read, Go, Fight, Win! and Go Indians! Along the parade route, people lined the streets, waving and cheering. Children from the nearby elementary school were dismissed from classes with their teachers in order to watch the parade.

The homecoming court led the parade. The girls were dressed in their elegant expensive gowns, riding in convertible sports cars that were donated by individuals and automobile dealerships in the community. Balloons and streamers were tied to everything and were everywhere. Children of all ages stood beside their parents, smiles shining wide across their faces, as if they were imagining themselves in the homecoming court. The girls riding in the convertibles waved as they passed the crowds. Their beauty was spotlighted as they experienced their forty-five minutes of fame and royalty as Bainesville's best. The expressions on the faces of the girls that they were taken by the moment awed as much of the waving children on the sidewalks as by the moment itself. When the parade was over, there was a scurry of activity in an attempt to maneuver the buses around all the vehicles that had been in and around the parade route. In a very few minutes, the kids were gone and the last bus had pulled away; and as thoughts turned toward the game, the day was over.

The weekly paper headlined an article about the upcoming homecoming game and had achieved their best start in several years. Optimism was running high. Game time was eight o'clock, pre-game festivities began at seven, and fans began arriving at six.

The first half of the game ended with the Indians ahead by ten points. The Indian football team had played well, looking confident against a weaker opponent. They headed into the locker room to await the end of the homecoming festivities. The stadium was packed with people. Faces eagerly gazed down at the field as the shiny, bright convertibles carried the homecoming contestants around the field and then back to the fifty yard line where an escort awaited each girl. Soon, everyone was in place. Silence fell over the stadium. The runners-up were announced first, followed by the name of the new homecoming queen for 1996–97. Cheers could be heard all around. The football team, who had exited the field house a bit too early, positioned themselves in the far corner of the field, with all players resting on one knee. As the last of the homecoming court left the field, the team—like their Roman counterparts of old—ran once again onto the field and prepared for battle.

The fight was not over. "So many people had come to see us, and to see the homecoming court and queen; we couldn't let them down. We had to win that game," says a football player from a student group. The final score was Indians, 21 and Pulaski County, 6.

The November wind blew briskly from the north end of the stadium where many community members had gathered for one last chance of celebration. The Indians, going into the final game of the 1996–97 season, were only one game away from making the regional play-offs. The stadium was jammed with people. From the press box, the scene resembled a sea of gold and purple. Numerous fans had painted Indian heads or tomahawks on their faces and wore hats, coats, and sweaters, proudly displaying the school's colors of gold and purple. The pounding of the golden milk jugs and the cheering from the crowd were deafening. The Indian football team had not reached the play-offs since the early 1980's. Although the team had shown moments of mastery over the sport, their play had been inconsistent from game to game, winning games they were expected to lose and losing games they should had won easily. The coaches were baffled by inconsistency.

The most difficult thing has been getting the players to believe that they can win. It takes a different kind of thinking and mental preparation, and I don't think that these guys have been taught how to do that. (Ben Mason, head football coach)

The Indians found themselves in a position to advance to the regional play-offs, but they would have to win their last regularly scheduled game of the season. It was a home game but against a tough opponent, and the team would have to play exceptionally well to get the victory that was needed to reach the play-offs.

"The thing that struck me the most about the last game of the season was that everything was in our favor. So what if we had only won three games? We only needed to win the last one to get to the play-offs. I knew that it was a long shot, but I had no idea how much a long shot it was. The kids didn't know how to get the job done. We have a lot more work to do here than I first thought, but we'll get there." (Ben Mason, head football coach)

In the end, the Indians fell short of the win, finishing the season with three wins and seven losses, still a tremendous improvement over the two previous seasons. The parents and fans maintained their support and involvement. One teacher described that it had been their hope and faith that the team would win some of the games. One parent remarked: "Football is just a big part of life in Bainesville. And when they [the football team] lose, that's when they need our support. I think it's important for them to know that we parents and everybody are behind them regardless if they win or lose." (Parent and community member)

With the final seconds' ticking off the clock, some of the players began to cry, realizing that the chance of making the play-offs had slipped away. Some threw their helmets to the ground in frustration. In the stands, parents wiped tears from their eyes. The golden jugs were replaced by tissues. One board member remarked, "We'll get 'em next year. We had a pretty good season and the boys (the football players) played hard all year. We'll get 'em next year." An hour after the game was over; the stadium went dark as the bright stadium lights signaling Friday night football were switched off. The parking lot was empty except for the cars of a few of the players and their friends who stood talking, probably replaying some missed block or a pass that should have been caught. As the lights of the stadium went dark, another year of Indian football was history.

In addition to the football games, bonfires, and parades, the Bainesville community also celebrates its heritage by hosting several annual festivals and craft shows. These include Gold Rush Days, which celebrates the gold discovered here in 1828; the Wild Flower Festival, a celebration of flowers and crafts; and the Bear on the Square Festival, a celebration only two years old that pays tribute to the rich natural environment of the area.

The Bear on the Square Festival is based on a true story. A few years ago, a small black bear wandered into town and climbed a tree adjacent to the town square. Apparently frightened by his position and altitude in the tree, the bear chose to remain in the tree overnight. Officials from the

State Department of Natural Resources were called in, and with the help of many local people, they rescued and relocated the bear. In the weeks preceding the festival, posters of the bear in the tree are found on nearly every bulletin board in town as well as in store windows and on utility poles. The festival brings a generous supply of music, dancing, singing, and a generally festive atmosphere. It is a time of celebration and of coming together as the community did during the original "bear on the square" crisis.

Acts of coming together in celebration and festivity are also present within the school culture, particularly in the fall of the year during football season. Planning for the activities and events related to these celebrations becomes an additional channel for social interaction and cohesion. By "coming together," the community also illustrates its commitment to preserve and sustain their culture. The survival of the school culture at Bainesville High

School is rooted in and built around the school's athletic program, specifically football.

Chapter Nine

Only the Strong Survive

Survival of the School Culture

The school culture at Bainesville High School is one of survival—both in the day-to-day activities that fill the school year and in the symbols, rituals, and ceremonies that are recognized and revered from year to year and from generation to generation. The Indian spirit, a symbolic and metaphoric connection to the ancestry of the area, is a major aspect of the school culture. School yearbooks, dating back to 1952, reflect a theme tied to the Native American culture. Titles such as "We Will Not Go Quietly," (referencing the forced exodus of the Cherokee in the early 1840s), "The Strength Is in the Tribe," and "To the Beat of a Different Drum," reinforce the role of Native American myth and spirit in the day-to-day activities of the school. The 1971 yearbook opens with a two-page spread of pictures showing an empty hallway, an empty classroom, a barren football field, and the remnants of the burnt wood used for the bonfire. The pictures are inscribed with the words, "Our World without people is a barren hallway, a vacant room, a deserted football field and an unlit bonfire" (1971 *Argus*, Bainesville High School, 2, 3).

The research question suggests that there is a connection among the school culture, the community's involvement with the school, and the school's athletic programs—specifically, in this case, Bainesville Indian football. Tangible evidence of such connections and influences among these three components is illustrated through the existence of the symbols of the school, which are embraced by the community. These symbols, which are tangible carriers of the traditions and mores of the school's athletic culture, and also serve as emotional connectors for the various community members who choose to participate in the school's athletic events, are highlighted and illuminated throughout the language of the school. The yearbook solidifies the significance of the school's symbols, traditions, and rituals and secures their timeless value. Although their importance may vary, each symbol and tradition serves a unique and vital role in the survival of the school culture.

The identified symbols of the school (i.e., the rock, the totem pole, the Indian statue, and the *Argus* yearbook) and t he encased football jerseys enshrining the memory of former students are all highly significant to the high school culture and its connections with the community. The elements of homecoming week—the parade of floats through town, the bonfire the night before the game, and the homecoming game itself—all represent a connection to the past as well as a symbolic front-row seat for viewing the future. As these events are reenacted from year to year, they mark significant times on the high school's calendar and are recorded as athletic history within the school's yearbooks. The events themselves provide opportunities through which former students, parents, and other community members can join together in reaffirming their loyalty to and pride in the school. These events become the school's rituals and thus project a sort of social magic that is centered on human emotion. Perhaps Robert Fulghum summed it up most accurately when he said, "The ritual event sometimes results in that which is hoped for: a sense of reconnection—of belonging" (69). In Bainesville, participation in the high school's athletic programs and events—whether as a fan, a parent, a student, or a player—allows one to engage in the fantasy of reconnecting to the past, of remembering.

Symbolic ties to the school and its history are many. The school sign that stands just outside the front entrance reads, Bainesville High School, Home of the Mighty Indians. On a wall in the high school gym, a prominent mural depicts an Indian warrior crashing through a wall of cinder blocks. The message reads: Welcome to Indian Territory. Beware! A large wooden billboard, adjacent to the concrete bleachers in the football stadium, bears the title: Indian Spirit Board. Names of businesses that support the Bainesville Indian athletic program dot the billboard. This serves as an instant reminder of their community pride and perhaps clout. The school's history is connected to the community. Robert Fulghum (1995) referred to the importance and use of symbols as "the physical signs of relationships with people and places and experiences." He also noted that the enactment of rituals and ceremonies of an organization or group "is a symbol of connection and reconnection, union and reunion with what is sacred to us" (88).

The survival of the school's culture can also be found in the verbiage used by cheerleaders, athletes, coaches, staff members, and administrators, who are the keepers of the school spirit. Glancing through the school's yearbooks, one can cite quotes from coaches that are indicative of the school's culture and connection to its past: "The fighting Indian spirit led us to victory," or "The team played with great enthusiasm and spirit against Gibson." Captions beneath photos of the student body at a football game or pep rally are similar, reading, "Go Indians Catch the Spirit," or "Seniors Have Spirit." An excerpt from the 1990 *Argus* reads:

> SPIRIT. What exactly is it in our school that has caused such uproar? It's a little thing called spirit, and without it a school can't survive. It seems to be taking over everyone this year. It is now obvious that a change has taken place, and it is showing in the faces of all the students. A short walk across the bridge or down the hall will prove that. The spirit of the fans has filled the stands at games and assemblies and has shaken the gym with cheers. (5)

The survival of school spirit and school culture is closely linked together. Through their participation in the various activities related to the football season, members of the school community—including students, parents, and others who are supportive—ensure the connection between the school's culture and its spirit. By participating in the rituals and ceremonies of school activities, they have taken ownership of the moment; they have become part of the memory and part of the excitement, enthusiasm, and the sometimes euphoric feeling recognized as school spirit. According to Tom Driver (1991, 35), "Ritualization becomes morally significant and necessary for group survival . . . since rituals provide channeling and moderation." The athletes, cheerleaders, coaches, and sponsors are keepers of the spirit—a spirit of survival. And a renewal of this enthusiasm for the school is passed on from class to class, year after year.

The community also plays an important role in keeping the school spirit thriving. Their attendance at games, pep rallies, and assemblies are direct examples of their support and enthusiasm. Some members of the community, however, respond in more subtle and less public ways. When I asked a group of former students how the community demonstrated support for the school's athletes and athletic programs, a student who was a cheerleader and soccer player responded: "In the *Nuggett* (the local weekly paper), when we had our picture in there, the president of the ban sent me a copy of the picture and wrote, "Congratulations!" on it. That was a way of showing support, of showing that he cares."

The rituals and ceremonies observed throughout the school year serve as the trusses of the school culture, designed to support and reinforce the values and beliefs held by all those who identify themselves as Bainesville Indians. Ceremonies like one that takes place during halftime of the last home football game and recognizes the senior athletes, band members, and cheerleaders, along with their parents or closest relatives, reinforce the values of family and the importance of being a part of a community. This holds true both within the school culture and in the community at large. The festivities of the homecoming game and all that precedes the game are also examples of the value placed on time-honored rituals and ceremonies, such as the bonfire and the ritualistic burning of the effigy of the opponent's mascot. Rituals that are ceremonious—such as the retiring of the jersey of a student athlete who has died, the kidnapping and relocating of the Indian statue for the graduation ceremony, or the touching the Indian's arm by each senior as he/she begins marching into the future, reflect important pieces of the school culture. Athletics, and the activities associated with athletic events, are major channels through which the cultural language of the school can be expressed. Although rituals and ceremonies represent only a part of the language of school culture, it is a critical part, indeed.

Adherence to and recognition of the school's traditions and rituals depend on the actions of those who respond to the enactment of these traditions, rituals, and ceremonies. The high school's athletics are interwoven with the symbols of the school, becoming a featured element in the tapestry of the school's culture. The enactment of and participation in ceremonies and celebrations surrounding school events provide the glue for creating cohesion among members of the group, school, and community. It is not necessarily the ceremony or celebration that is most significant, but the participation in the event that adds distinction and reverence to its existence.

Rituals that occur at a prescribed rate of frequency are given significance and importance by the values and beliefs held by the school and community. These take on an almost mystical value or power as they reinforce historical traditions and mores. While rituals and ceremonies are primarily demonstrations of the act of remembering, they also reinforce the importance of the person, the belief, or the tradition being celebrated within the community or the school. In the Bainesville community, citizens demonstrate their values and beliefs about the importance of participating as spectators and fans by their attendance at games and other school-related activities. Bonfires and football games against rival teams exemplify these rituals of remembering, the art of projecting one's hopes and dreams into a celebration with jubilant song and dance and talk about a possible victory the next evening.

Ceremonies, in contrast, illuminate the style in which the rituals are enacted or carried out. The ceremony provides the eloquence for the ritual or celebration. Additionally, it is the ceremony of the events—of the ritual—that summons the spirit of unity. And it is the spirit of unity that ignites the hopes and dreams, hence, the emotions for those who are connected with the school. As demonstrated by the Bainesville community, the rituals of ceremony and celebration are necessary to realign, reaffirm, and refocus the values and beliefs of the people within the school and community. They provide pageantry, gala, recognition, and reflection. Renewal ignites the hearts and souls of the individuals within the community.

A sense of the spirit of unity permeates the stories of the people of Bainesville—stories about their school, their sports teams, and the community. Their stories are filled with joy and hope, happiness and sadness. They demonstrate a willingness to imagine the triumph that provides strength necessary for perseverance that is evident in their actions, thoughts, and comments. In speaking about the activities that occur within the school, from the drama productions to the pep rallies and football games, the high school principal summed it up, "It's (the high school) the heart of the community; a source of pride, both for our students and teachers as well as parents and others in the community. It provides energy for the community." The energy referred to by the school principal is demonstrated through the actions and attitudes of the community's citizens.

High school athletic events at Bainesville High School represent celebrations of community culture. The rituals and ceremonies associated with the school, and its sporting events help develop the social values and social mores of the community. High school athletics, specifically high school football, provides a conduit through which the community's expression of celebration can be heard. The football games offer repeated occasions for social interaction among all members of the community. Conversations, mostly focused on the football program or closely related events, keep the hearts and minds of those closely connected with the school's athletic program pumping with enthusiasm, frustration, and sometimes even anger; but sometimes the conversations stray, becoming opportunities to discuss and debate small town politics or spread the latest gossip. The people of

Bainesville High School—students, players, teachers, and parents alike—are passionate about their football team. The community members who attend games rally in support, encouraging the players to struggle through their defeats, to gain the extra yards, and to tackle a little harder. The community's support and determination become even more entrenched when the team experiences losses.

The 1996–97 season was no different. In fact, the performance of the football team was similar. They began the season with a game against their biggest rival and ended the season with an overall record of four wins and six losses (4–6). During their first game, a hero emerged in number 21, a running back that was a senior on the football team and a leader both on the field and within the school—well respected by his coaches, teachers, students and community. He was stocky and strong, and his greatest observable attributes were his desire to run the football and his enthusiasm and excitement in reaction to his own exceptional performance. His determination defined his character, and the fans—the community—noticed and began to celebrate his presence on the field. As the season wore on, signs proclaiming his number and name appeared more and more frequently in the stands.

Another example of the community pulling together was observed during the 1997–98 football season. The fans, through an emerging process of cheering and responding, selected their "hero of the year," a football player who became the focal point of their enthusiasm. As the season progressed, the support and excitement for the player dubbed as the hero grew. This support became readily evident by the presence of banners in the stands and the resounding cheers from the fans. One small group I observed during an away game, with the temperature well below thirty-five degrees and as rain began to fall, stood on the top row of the bleachers with a bed sheet stretched out and held high, which read, "Coach, we want number 28. Run number 28." The rest of the fans joined them in their cheers and called for number 28.

Number 28 was a sophomore and was not a starter but a backup runner. The few times he had been sent in and given the chance to run the ball, he did so with such determination and excitement that the crowd went crazy. After every carry, number 28, who was not as big as most of the other players, literally jumped to his feet and ran back to the huddle. Whenever he made an exceptional run, gaining several yards, he leapt with enthusiasm, raising his arms high in celebration. If he was substituted, the fans booed and then began to chant his name. This occurred on numerous occasions and mostly when the team was losing or was behind by several touchdowns. Perhaps, with the team losing more games than it won, it made the struggle more tolerable. To find a hero—a player who gave them hope and purpose, a player who helped them believe that winning was possible— and to celebrate this player's efforts was possibly an exercise in loyalty. The new hero, like most of the young men on the football team, came from a hardworking middle-class family. Each time he ran the ball and turned up field with a burst of speed and determination, the crowd stood and cheered. His mother, raising her arms in the air, would shout his name and scream, "Way to go, son! That's my boy!"

Coming together to watch the football game created fervor of excitement as the fans applauded their momentary hero. For the home team and its heroes, the community renewed its faith and allegiance to the school and created new memories.

The golden jugs had emerged during the 1996–97 football season as rallying symbols had carried over to the 1997–98 season. It was the night of the 1997 homecoming bonfire when the jugs reappeared. They were there the next day at the pep rally and again at the homecoming game. Someone had taken gallon milk jugs, painted them gold, and had written slogans and symbols on the sides of them and put a handful of rocks inside. Several of the golden jugs had the numbers of certain players painted on them. The golden jugs, used as noisemakers, became a symbol of the renewed enthusiasm for the football team.

One of the cheerleaders expressed it this way: "Well, we made about fifty million milk jugs (laughter). I think how it got started was we had some paint left over, and we decided to paint some. We had them at the pep rally on Friday of the homecoming game. Then, they started showing up everywhere. The idea caught on, and the parents got involved. And more and more, everybody had a gold milk jug. The sound was loud whenever they would shake them."

The school principal, seated behind her desk for an interview with me, gazed up toward the ceiling in reflective thought as she offered her perspective on the golden jugs, their significance, and how they got started: "One highlight I remember was toward the end of the football season this year.

Some creative mother painted some milk jugs gold and filled them with rocks and put Indian symbols on them and wrote some phrases. And to me, to see people in the stands standing up with the milk jugs in their hands shaking them and rattling all those rocks when you made a pass or a few yards, or just when you had the ball, that was an exciting time. People were standing up to see and be supportive of the team. So we only went 3–7, which was just a small margin of success from the previous year. But in the spirit of the competition, it was a much larger success I believe." (Carla Jenette, principal)

Looking out from the press box, high above the stands and the crowd, the jugs formed a sea of gold as the fans stood and cheered and waved them. The sound they made was thunderous. Appropriately, it was like an Indian war chant, performed in unison.

Connection between the community and Bainesville High School athletics is maintained through the ritual of remembering through participation in the high school's athletic events. Robert Fulghum (1995, 51) postulates that "Personal events contain the universal themes that tie us to humanity, past, present, and future. The ritual is in the remembering—the remembering is self-revelation." Everything about the high school experience, to some degree, is held in memory. It seems that now, following the 1996 and 1997 football seasons, a new memory has been added to the long list of those that are already part of the Indian football tradition; now there are the golden jugs! The golden jugs, gallon milk bottles, or jugs, painted gold with purple numbers of various players on them, represented the war-cry of the Bainesville Indians. The state high school athletic association had forbidden the use of cow-bells at the ballgames, which was quickly replaced by the "golden jugs" filled with rocks, that sounded like thunder on a country road.

Chapter Ten

History and Politics of Bainesville Football

Athletics and sporting events are major parts of life at Bainesville High School and serve as common ground between families and the community. This is evidenced by the amount of emphasis parents place on Friday night football and the high school's football program. In fact, from the time children are old enough to play Little League baseball or peewee football, parents play an active role. It is not surprising in such a community that middle school and high school athletics continue to serve as forums for parent involvement. The events, festivities, and activities associated with the high school athletic culture assume a symbolic role in shaping and affecting the lives of students and parents. These activities become conduits for interaction and unity and are embedded in the school's culture and carried out faithfully each year.

The football program began in the fall of 1960. A. P. Kennon was the high school principal in 1960 and was largely responsible for starting the football program. Bainesville's football stadium is named in his honor. The Bainesville Indians played only five games during their first year of competition and ended the season with a win/loss record of three wins and two losses. The Indian's next winning season was in the fall of 1963 when they played ten games and won six. Bainesville football teams have amassed a total of 126 wins, 237 loses, and 10 ties, with a total of fourteen different head coaches during the program's thirty-eight years of existence.

Bainesville football is a highly political and highly volatile issue in the community. The football program at Bainesville High School, along with the Bainesville community, experienced two major coaching crises: one in the summer of 1994 and another in the spring of 1995. Both controversies involved the coaching staff at the high school and created anger, animosity, and frustration among the community members, students, players, and other school personnel. Some have said that the coaching controversies of 1994 and 1995 were major setbacks for the high school football program, such that it will take years to completely recover.

The first coaching crisis came in the summer of 1994. Coach Joe Floyd had been at the helm for three years and was about to begin his fourth season at Bainesville High School. Although Floyd was not from the Bainesville area, he and his family had been adopted by the community. On the first day of summer football camp, with Coach Floyd and his assistant coaches finalizing their plans for the first practice session, the unthinkable happened. An unfamiliar car drove into the parking lot. An unknown person emerged from the car and walked over to the group of coaches, who by then were almost gawking at the stranger dressed in what appeared to be coaching attire. The stranger walked up to the group and introduced himself as Sam Bradshaw, the newly hired head football coach. From that point forward, the football season of 1994 was overshadowed by the biggest coaching controversy that had ever hit Bainesville.

The local paper became a megaphone for discontent during the coaching controversy as various community members waged war against each other, plotting their attacks and counterattacks in a public forum. Letters to the editor of the *Bainesville Nuggett* reflected a range of opinions and attitudes toward the high school football program, the administration, and the coaches involved.

In the end, Coach Floyd and all of his assistant coaches would resign after coaching the Bainesville Indians for three seasons; and Sam Bradshaw, with the eventual help from the community, would take over the summer football camp and the coaching duties of the 1994 season.

The second coaching crisis for the high school football program came in the spring of 1995, on the heals of the double-head coach ordeal. Sam Bradshaw did not have his contract renewed, despite pleas from the community. Bradshaw had replaced Floyd at the beginning of the 1994–95 season.

As one observer put it, "In the April 13, 1995, issue of the *Bainesville Nuggett*, an article appeared announcing that the Bainesville Board of Education had voted not to renew coach Bradshaw's contract for the following year. Then, at the next board meeting, an article appeared in the newspaper saying that a contract for another new coach had been approved for the 1995–96 football season."

Jay Thomas had accepted the head-coaching position at Bainesville High School, following the controversy of 1994. It was his first head-coaching job, and it would not be pleasant. Jay Thomas had been a football coach for more than fifteen years;

but his personality was that of a quite, shy, and unassuming character. When asked about the 1995–96 football season when Coach Thomas came aboard, Mrs. Jenette, Bainesville High School principal, made the following observation, noting that the newly hired Coach Thomas had walked into a politically hot situation at the outset, implying that things went downhill from there. Under Coach Thomas, the Indians lost every game they played.

The politics [about the football situation] in the community played a very heavy part. The parents were looking for immediate change and gratification. When the wins didn't happen, there were factions that wanted to get rid of the coach or coaches within two or three games. They were ready to cut their losses and go. I think that when parents become disgruntled, and their whole attitude toward the school . . . It seems as though nothing can be done correctly.

A review of the school's football history and records illustrates the struggle and frustration the school and community have endured. Since the early 1960s, the win-loss record of the Bainesville Indians has reflected the inconsistency and controversy that still surround the football program today. In an odd sort of way, the community demonstrates a sense of unity, although it resembles a "united rebellion" whenever they perceive a crisis or controversy to be threatening the football program or the players.

Two examples of such political crisis and community controversy concerning the high school football program occurred in 1994 and 1996. The first was in the fall of 1994 when the "great coach controversy," as it was called, erupted. The second crisis occurred in 1995 when the football team went 0 and 10 for the season. The stories told about these critical times serve as illustrations of the community struggling, yet pulling together, in a commitment to the young men who play the game of football.

Chapter Eleven

The Great Coaching Controversy

The tangled chain of events began in July 1994, just prior to the planning of summer football camp for the players at Bainesville High School. Coach Jim Floyd had completed three years as the head coach for the Bainesville Indians and was about to begin a fourth season. Although, his win/loss record was a dismal 4–25–1, the community appeared optimistic.

The superintendent of schools, who had been a teacher at Bainesville High School prior to his election (to the office of the superintendent), in collaboration with the high school principal, decided to make a change in the football coaching staff at the high school. As time drew near for the start of the August football camp, the high school had a problem—it had *two* head football coaches.

"One guy would have been back for his fourth year," said Coach Floyd.

"He had already signed a contract. Then, we had another guy," Said Sam Bradshaw, "to show up from Jacksonville, Florida, who had a verbal agreement with the superintendent, but no contract. So it comes time to start summer practice." Coach Floyd shows up, and the new coach shows up. And the assistant coaches, they show up. Coach Floyd (the old head coach) realizes what has happened, so he goes over to the superintendent's office and resigns," said S. Reeves, teacher.

Glenn Reynolds, who was the athletic director during the 1994–95 season, recalled: "I saw it, both head coaches showed up. The players didn't know what to do. I think they eventually went back inside the locker room and took their pads and stuff off. Hell, it was a fiasco, boy! They (the coaches) were shouting at each other. I thought we were going to have a fight. The next thing I know, we have this all-night board meeting. And I mean there was a crowd there. People were mad!"

Pam Donovan, one of the parents reflected: "The year that the coaching staff walked out, the kids went in the weight room, sat down, and cried. The whole dad-blamed football team was sitting there squalling because they didn't have a coach. Nothing but the [new] head coach was left. Every assistant coach and Coach Floyd had resigned."

Nancy Bowles, a parent of one of the cheerleaders, expressed her concerns regarding the coach controversy: "The situation was terrible, and of course, the students were upset about Coach Floyd leaving. He was well respected in the school."

Support for Coach Floyd was widespread across the county, as was indicated in the local newspaper. The headlines in the *Bainesville Nuggett* on August 4, 1994, read: COACHES QUIT! SPORTS PROGRAM IN CHAOS.

Parents were noted in the article as having said:

"The current situation is total chaos," Recalled a concerned parent.

"The coaches are fine men, but I don't agree with people walking out and leaving kids," said a concerned school administrator.

"We have a football season about to begin. Coach Floyd brought these kids along all these years. He was telling everyone in town, this year was going to be Bainesville's year. I think we should have left the program in place," remarked a concerned parent.

In the editorial section of the local paper, one parent remarked: "I think the solution is very plain and simple. We need to bring Coach Floyd back. He graced our kids as well as our community. He continues to support them and speak to them. I think we need to get him back here and get back

on the right track and win some ball games."
(*Bainesville Nugget*, August 11, 1994)

Other parents wrote to express their feelings
and opinions about Coach Floyd. Their comments
were very direct, brief, and to the point. Numerous
comments appeared in the editorial section of the
paper with titles such as "Floyd Was Best," "Floyd
Needed," "Solution Is Plain and Simple," "Parents
Want Old Coach Back," and "Mom Agrees," which
read: "As a mother of a football player, I'd like to
see Coach Floyd to be reconsidered to be hired
because he really cared. Floyd was about to begin
his fourth year as Bainesville's head football coach,
was well thought of in the community, and had
gained the respect of many—including players,
coaches, and community members. "

One former player described his relationship
with the coach: He was like a father figure to me.
He would talk with me after practice and explain
the plays and drills we had been working on during
practice. At times, I would be all tense and

frustrated; and after talking with Coach Floyd, I would be relaxed and ready to go. "He would also help me with my schoolwork and with problems I was having in school. He was just a great guy. I really felt bad for him," Austin Tolbert, former Bainesville football player.

Word about what had happened quickly spread through the community and through the conversations at places like the Spinning Wheel Restaurant, located two blocks from the school, Lucy's Cafe, and the Daybreak Cafe. "After I heard what had happened, I went straight to the field house where the football players were. Some had already gone home. But the players who were still there were very upset. I looked around, and my god, they were crying like babies. That just sent cold chills through me. Then, I got angry. They had no right to hurt those boys like that," said Louis Roundhouse, a parent of one of the players.

By the next afternoon, as a result of all of the assistant coaches resigning, some of the fathers of the players had made arrangements to work with the football team and the newly hired Sam Bradshaw as a community coaches, known as "lay coaches." They were determined not to allow the players to become victims of the political fighting occurring between the superintendent and the coaches.

The superintendent moved quickly to put into place coaches for the football team. The local newspaper chronicled the events:

> During the August 11–called meeting, the board (Bainesville Board of Education) decided to move forward with the certification of lay or community coaches to fill the needs of the [football] program. According to Lucas (the superintendent of Bainesville schools), he gave Glenn the authority to put the assistant coaches in place. (*Bainesville Nuggett*, August 18, 1994)

Fathers employed locally were given special consideration with flexible schedules; practice began at 3:15 every afternoon except for game day. Their labor of love, along with the newly hired head football coach, earned the football team three wins, six losses, one tie, and the respect of the community. The parents' involvement as community coaches clearly illustrates the importance placed on athletics in the Bainesville community.

The coaching controversy provided a spark for the community to unite and come together for a single cause—the football team and their coach. Coach Floyd had been well accepted into the community, which was illustrated by the reactions and comments of parents and other community leaders when Floyd was replaced. With the hiring of Sam Bradshaw, the community rose to the occasion in defense of someone who seems to care about their kids, their school, and their football program. They had, in turn, accepted Sam Bradshaw as their football coach and began to look past the ugly ordeal of 1994 as the football team finished the season with three wins, six losses, and one tie. In the spring of 1995, the school board decided not to renew Sam Bradshaw's contract.   The community once again was about to face another coaching ordeal as another new coach, Jay Thomas, was hired for the 1995–96 season.

Chapter Twelve

The 0-10 Season

As the 1995 season began, the parents were puzzled and frustrated with the new coach, Jay Thomas, because he had not asked for any input or help from them. Parent involvement had been a tradition with the football team, and they were determined to hold on to their role with the football program. Over the years, the role of the parents and other community members had emerged as one of nurturer, provider, and protector of the football team. What seemed to matter the most was how much the coach and his staff cared about the players. The parents and community members, in taking on their roles as supporter and protector of the football team, kept a watchful eye on the interactions of the players and coaches. Their roles varied. Some parents watched the practice sessions while other parents prepared the meals or provided extra transportation. Active participation, therefore, was an expectation of the community as well as a tradition. Failure to recognize the importance and necessity of the parents' and community members' participation was a grievous error on the part of the new head football coach. During the 1995 football season, many such errors were made.

"There was total support for the players. We fed them every . . . We all took turns—any time that we have helped with anything with the football program, it has been at the request of the coach. There was no input from Thomas (the coach during 1995–96 season) at all for any parent about anything he needed for the football team. There was no request for help from him. When we thought—realized—that he had no plans to feed them (the football team, before the home game), we took turns bringing in food before each home game," said Pam Donovan, parent.

Providing the pre-game meal and being involved with the football program in a supportive mode had been a tradition for parents from year to year. Word soon spread that the new coach was not including the parents and was not asking the parents for any help. This exclusion was a violation of traditions, rituals, and norms and caused some of the parents to become suspicious of the motives and the level of commitment of the new football coach.

The year (1995–96) began in conflict for Coach Thomas and only became worse. The Bainesville Indians lost their opening game against Dawkins County, their most noted rival. As the losses mounted, the frustration and anger from the community grew louder and more disturbing. Carla Jenette, the high school principal, recalled the atmosphere that surrounded the 1995–96 football season: "It was drudgery for them to get through that season. There was no excitement in the air, no anticipation. It was a job to go out and get done. There was some internal bickering, some quarrelsome-type things that would not have arisen had we been in a winning mode."

"A good example of that fact is that we had only one pep rally because it was so disastrous. Nobody cheered. Even the football players themselves . . . It was almost as though they were embarrassed to appear before the student body. The student body was not . . . They were polite, but they were certainly not engaged in the pep rallies or the games. They just sat there. There was no pride. There was nothing to be proud of, and there was no energy that was a product of that sports season at all," she said, finishing her thoughts on the matter.

The football players also felt the impact of the students' and community members' reactions and attitudes. A former football player who played on the 1995–96 team remembered: "Not winning any games made us feel like we weren't doing what we should have been doing. It made a lot of people think that we shouldn't be out there because we weren't playing to the best of our ability. And another thing, our seniors . . . I felt so bad for them. It was their last year, and we couldn't give them a winning season, not even a win, so . . . It was hard," as was told by a former player and dedicated fan of the Indians.

Although the parents were angry and they had serious disagreement with the coach, they supported the players. The parents and relatives of the football players, as well as other community members, committed themselves to showing up for the games, regardless of the outcome. This commitment from the community, from parents of athletes and non-athletes, emerged as one of the strongest attributes of the Bainesville community. When asked about why attendance at the (football) games had been consistently high over a long period of time, Adam Boatwright explained that attending the Friday night football games was as much a part of life in Bainesville as going down to the post office or the grocery store.

It's the topic of conversation. Wherever you go, (football) is the enthusiasm that is in the community. Everybody just kind of keeps up; and of course, being a small community, people know most of the athletes.

The level of parental support and community commitment, however, has roots that run deeper than just that of entertainment value. The root of support, enthusiasm, and commitment demonstrated through attendance at football games—even in the face of defeat—acts as a mirror of the community, providing a reflection of itself regardless of age or time. When the football team was struggling through a game, with the cheers and yells projected forward toward the playing field where the warriors were doing battle, the fans were transcended in time. It can be said that everyone loves and follows a winner, but Bainesville football has lost more games than it has won since the inaugural season in the fall of 1960. Still, the fans—the community, consisting of parents of athletes, business people, alumni, and other adults, both young and old—have become avid followers, supporters, and, indeed, believers in Bainesville Indian football.

"They still remember [when they were in high school] whether they played or not, that it was their team on the field, and they felt a part of it. It's just as much like the alumni of a four-year school (college). They're alumni of their high school. And I think they go back [to the games] for that reason. They still feel a part of the school where they graduated or attended, even if they didn't graduate," according to Adam Boatwright, teacher and community member.

Commitment through Struggle

One parent noted that on any given Friday night during the 1995 football season, the stands were packed—standing room only. Game attendance was as much a Friday night ritual as being able to see the lights of the stadium from the town square on Friday nights in the fall of the year.

Amid controversy and struggle, the community responded on game nights. "The numbers were pretty good. It was a god-awful start for the football team that year, but I couldn't tell a difference in fan support. Yeah, there was division in the community. But people showed up for the games," said S. Reeves, teacher.

"They went to school here, and now their children go here, and, although their children may not play any sports, they come to watch," said Michelle Smith, a teacher and community member. The observation from Michelle Smith amplified the sentiment in the community and reflected the amount of support that existed in the community for the Bainesville High School football team.

Steven Riley, a native Bainesvillian, framed it this way: "Bainesville has not changed tremendously over the years. A lot of people still enjoy going out to the [football] ball games simply because it gets them out of the house; a lot of it has to do with getting out and socializing with people. Still, you have others who are reliving their past, playing days through their kids, wanting them to be more successful than they were."

According to Shirley Dillard, a teacher and native Bainesvillian, "people attend the high school football games because they are supporters of the football team and they want to cheer for their team.."

A lot of people attended because they had somebody related to them out there playing. And then, a lot of people attended who were just supporters of the team. They were there; and they hoped that by having their body there and by cheering, they could do something to motivate, to inspire, to encourage the kids who were taking a beating. Kids were suffering. Kids seemed to be getting it from every side. They were getting it from their parents . . . from their coaches . . . from the town . . . from other teams. And so, people showed up just because they felt sorry, in some cases. And they showed up because, you know, everybody likes to cheer the underdog.

The end of the 1995–96 school year came slowly, and everyone looked to the next August for a chance to renew their hopes and dreams of a winning football team. They would begin with a new coach and a new coaching staff and, again, full support from the Bainesville High School Booster Club. The 1996 August football camp finally arrived.

* * * * * * * * *

Certain prevailing themes framed each interview conducted during this study, and these same themes were present in the various activities and celebrations observed during the research period. There is strong connectivity between the members of the community, both native members and adopted members and the school, particularly with athletics—specifically with football. The school's history with the sport of football, as well as some of the other sports sponsored by the high school, reflects a high level of involvement from both the school and community. Even though during its thirty-seven-year history the football team has never sustained consecutive winning seasons where the team won five or more games during the season, community support and involvement with the activities of the game have been transformed into that of tradition. The sport of football and all that is associated with it has prompted political fights, turf-guarding maneuvers between various community leaders including school administration, and a sense of unity in the midst of conflict and controversy. The football team and the Friday night home games are not only major community activities of the fall season, but they represent tradition and loyalty. The home football stadium is the symbolic stage for the Bainesville community, whereby the one-act plays and yearly sequels are played before the community, with various members of the community, school administration, and/or school board members starring in leading roles. The symbols of the school—such as the Indian, the high school mascot; the totem pole outside the gymnasium; and the rock, used by students and teachers to announce the latest slogans; team scores as well as encouragement from the community—are the everyday reminders to the community that their school has life and spirit. Other symbols of school spirit and enthusiasm emerged as the season progressed. Like torches in the night leading the way, once a symbol of enthusiasm was introduced, such as the golden jugs filled with rocks, they became the rallying cry of the fans. Perhaps Robert Fulghum summed it up most accurately, "The ritual event sometimes results in that which is hoped for: a sense of reconnection—of belonging" (69). For Bainesville, participation in the high school's athletic programs and events—whether as a fan, a parent, a student, or a player—provides an avenue and an opportunity for fantasy, for reconnecting with the past, and a chance to remember.

Chapter Thirteen

A Treasure Maintained?

You fall in love with this place—the panoramic views of the mountains, the town square, the people. It's kind of like going to somebody's house where you know it's okay to put your feet on the table because you feel at home. You feel comfortable. *(Steve Rhodes, community member and teacher)*

The Bainesville community has its share of conflict and controversy, which at times threatens the very survival of the community. The people of Bainesville, however, are committed to maintaining and protecting their way of life. Most people in the community have worked to preserve their self-sufficiency while maintaining a rural identity consisting of simple and basic values and beliefs and having a sense of pride in their community, their school, and their athletic programs. When asked about the Bainesville community, one teacher observed: It's a rural community where everybody knows most everybody. We don't have the big shopping malls and other things large metropolitan areas have, but we like it that way. Life is simple here. It's comfortable. The residents of Bainesville value and defend the notion of small town life as superior to that of the big city.

Bainesville High School and its athletic programs ignite an intense level of human emotion. Peshkin (1978, 193) wrote about the small town of Mansfield and its ethos, "the guiding belief . . . the spirit that motivates the ideas . . . or practices of a people." In a similar manner, Bainesville's ethos has been formed with the expectations of Bainesville football as paramount to the center of community.

Susan Diamonds, a native Bainesvillian and teacher, remarked, "When I was a student, (school) spirit was a living thing. We believed in our school.

We wore the purple and gold and we wore it proudly." Indeed, the entire community is involved during football season, from the purchasing of football programs and sweatshirts with BHS Indian logos to placing ads in the local newspaper encouraging the players to win.

The community comes together for the sake of the football team: they buy and sell tickets to the annual barbecue chicken dinner sponsored by the school's athletic booster club; and they line the streets, waving and clapping, as the homecoming parade progresses slowly through town. On certain Saturday mornings, the cheerleaders hold car washes to raise money for their trip to summer cheerleading camp, and people from all around the community line up in the student parking lot.

Comparatively, on Friday nights, they come to the games, dressed in purple and gold, ready to yell and scream for the Indian football team. There is a definite sense of belonging, of being a part of the community.

Football is also a source of community pride. Carla Jenette, the high school principal, reflected: "Football plays a very major role [in this community]. Most of these children have grown up together, and for most, it is a family tradition. You'll have families where their father and their grandfather played football here, and now their brothers and sisters are all involved in the athletic program."

Peshkin (1978, 45) remarked that a "football game is a significant social occasion, during which a variety of personal and community needs and feelings are satisfied and reinforced." Such family patterns, which appeared in the Bainesville community, affirm Peshkin's belief.

One thing is clear in the Bainesville community. The importance and value of the high school, regardless of status or condition, remain the central themes of the community, connected by a complex tapestry of social interaction. Acute familiarity between the various constituencies whose interactions overlap ensures the connections and relevance between and among the groups. According to Galbraith, "Rural youth and adults interact with the same people in multiple social settings; e.g., you see the same people at the market, at church, at work, and at school functions. Because of size, organizations can be less bureaucratic, communications tend to be verbal rather than written, who said it is as important as what's said" (74).

A Treasure Maintained?

The Bainesville community is isolated geographically from the many modern conveniences of the big city. Its very virtues are steeped in the traditions and history connected to the area. Teachers, administrators, board members, parents, and other community members have multiple and sometimes overlapping roles in the activities of the community, especially when these activities concern the school and specifically when they pertain to the high school's football program. The parents and other community constituents in Bainesville remain desirous of playing a major role and of holding a position in the organization of the football program that brings admiration and clout among their peers.

Data from this study closely parallel similar research that points to the fact that in small rural communities, the high school is the centerpiece. Alan Peshkin (1978) in his study of Mansfield, a rural community, noted that the school was the heart of the community. In her interview, Carla Jenette reiterated this point, stating that "Bainesville High School is the heart of the Bainesville community, and the football program probably ranks as high as church and work with many residents in this area."

The ways in which the community is connected and intertwined with the high school's football program and the school's culture illuminate a complex interdependent network of communication and social interaction. These interdependent networks seem timeless and are tightly and deeply woven into the culture. Revisiting the traditions of homecoming bonfires and opening game rivalries reaffirms the beliefs that, amid everyday life, the old school and the memories created long ago remain the centerpiece of the community. As one community member remarked, "Homecoming week is an important week, and the bonfire and parade are very important events for the community."

The roles and relationships among the residents of Bainesville that have been explored through this study support the understanding of rural Americans and their way of life, how their children are educated and why those who live in rural communities fight for their very survival. Dunne (1981) asserted that true "rural education" was not found in large rural schools and not even in all small schools. Real rural education, Dunne argued, was defined by these characteristically rural strengths: a lack of distinction between what belongs in school and what belongs in the community, a kind of generalization that expects people to do whatever they are able without filling specialized roles or performing strictly age-graded functions, close and supportive ties between families and schools, a sense of comfort and cooperative spirit among schoolchildren, and rural independence and self-reliance translated into the school setting (4). The ambiguity between the role and purpose of the school and the role and purpose of the community reinforces Dunne's assertions that "a sense of comfort and cooperative spirit" and the "lack of distinction of what belongs in the school and what belongs in the community" are in and of themselves a natural state of conflict. The intrusive nature exhibited by the parents, for example, during the great coaching controversy illustrates that parents will intervene when they feel the school and its football program are threatened, protecting an icon of their community.

The research from this study also suggests that through the participation of incongruent-conflict-type activities, members of the community find a sense of unity. Points of conflict become rallying cries.   Problems experienced around the school, therefore, take on a greater degree of significance in the life of a Bainesvillian.   Becoming involved with the problems or crises connected to the school provides an avenue for members of the community to share in the unity, to belong.   Schmuck and Schmuck (1989, 2) likened "the small town school to a vortex, drawing everyone into it and serving as a foundation for the community.   The school [in small rural towns] engages virtually everyone, regardless of age, because, like a river's eddy, it irresistibly draws the community's residents into it."

Inasmuch as the school is the heart of the community, it provides a stage for celebration. Bainesvillians celebrate their pride and loyalty to entities that through time have been tempered by tradition and ritual.   The celebrations manufactured and maintained within the confines of the school, draped in ceremony and pageantry, expand the parameters of ritual and tradition.   The community becomes involved with the process of the celebration, and thus, as adults and non-students, they become the ceremonial leaders of the celebration. As Deal and Peterson (1994, 8) noted, "Ceremonies are powerful community events that build identity, spirit, and commitment. The act of being involved with the planning and orchestrating of the events attached to a celebration reinforces the value and importance of the events. This process creates a cultural space, as described further by Deal and Peterson (1994, 89) in which stories are told, rituals are reenacted, and heroes and heroines are anointed. The ceremonies associated with school/athletic events (e.g., the planning of homecoming events, the homecoming parade, and the homecoming football game) become the prerequisites of the celebration. Ceremonies associated with Bainesville High School athletics, which carried out over a period of years, then become traditions and are expected to occur from year to year. Thus, the ceremonies and acts of celebration become rituals.

Chapter Fourteen

The Research Is Over, the Dissertation Is Written: Now What? So What?

The school leader is the keeper of the school spirit. School spirit refers to the enthusiasm and exuberance for the school, its athletic teams, its drama teams—everything that is symbolic of the school; it conjures up feelings of hope and joy for a positive future. The school leader's role, therefore, is to ensure that a high level of enthusiasm, and thus commitment, is conveyed to the various members of the school community. Fulfilling the role of keeper of the school spirit demands active participation and understanding of the school culture.

The role and existence of what has been referred to as "school spirit" or "community spirit" have significant influence within the Bainesville Community. The enthusiasm marked by each Friday night home football game is a demonstration of community spirit in support of school spirit, with the spirit most often referred to and invoked by those directly involved with the activities connected with the high school.

Community spirit—sometimes called enthusiasm, loyalty, and/or faithfulness—emerged during the study period as a fairly significant ingredient in the school's connection with the Bainesville community. An illustration of community spirit is seen in the ways the community has supported the Bainesville football team for thirty-seven years, even though the team has not been very successful. The community looks upon the players and their coaches as recipients of the community's guardianship. It is through participation in the activities connected with the school, specifically the football program that the community's spirit of unity collides with the notion of school spirit. Harrison Owen (1990, 2), in his work on the spiritual transformation and development of organizations, defined "spirit" as the "energy and flow," which drives the structure and form of organizations; in the case of Bainesville, the community is both the source and recipient of the energy and flow of organization, hence community spirit referred to by Owens. Owen labels the place in which spirit reveals itself, moves, transforms, and develops organizations [communities] as "mythos," comprised of "story and ritual" (12). Tom Driver (1991, 90) in *The Magic of Ritual,* noted that "rituals acquire mythical and symbolic interpretations in the course of time." The act of storytelling and the acting out of specific rituals and traditions associated with Bainesville High School football reinforce the myths and ethos that translate into expectations, loyalty, and pride. Carla Jenette, principal of Bainesville High School, echoed this sentiment in remarking that the high school and its football team are the heart and pride of the community. Understanding the role and implications of tradition, ritual, and ceremony, the spirit becomes essential for those who are employed as school administrators. Spirit is discernibly active in the Bainesville community through formal and informal ceremonies, events, and celebrations and in the stories that are told within the organization of the school and the boundaries of the community. Those stories and rituals can indeed be thought about, interpreted by, and experienced by the members within the school and community.

During the coaching controversy, the role and value of the school/community culture, its myths and ethos, along with the rituals and traditions connected with the football team were ignored. The results were anger and confusion. The balance between the mythical and symbolic elements of the

Bainesville High School football program and the actual administration and management of the school were cast in roles of disharmony. The actions and decisions of school administrators, coaches, the superintendent, and others from the community forced misalignment between the school spirit and community unity (community spirit). Hiring a new head football coach without the smooth exit of and disconnection with the previous coach caused emotional reactions from players, parents, and community supporters. The local weekly newspaper became the town crier, noting every move and statement by the local school board and publishing editorial comments from the community.

In contrast, the administration, hired in the summer of 1995, has taken steps in recognizing and reinforcing the value and role of the high school's traditions and rituals. Through the orchestration of activities associated with the football program (pep rallies to pre-game meals for the football players to recognizing the parents of seniors who participate in athletics at Bainesville High School), the school principal and school superintendent have made their symbolic statement regarding the school's traditions, rituals, and ceremonies. Their efforts to allow time for and recognition of the community's values and beliefs in school traditions have instilled a sense of teamwork, an esprit de corps among those who identify themselves as Bainesville High School Indians.

For school administrators, the study of the role of high school athletics in rural communities outlines the need for a clear and complete understanding of the relationship between that of social interaction at high school athletic events and the cultivation of community spirit and unity. In some school systems, the success of the football team, for example, sometimes determines the length of tenure of not only the football coach, but also the tenure and success of the school principal and the school superintendent. Those who serve as members of the local board of education are the very persons, in the eyes of the community, who make the decisions that affect the children of the community. They are the same people who increase taxes, approve the purchase of textbooks, approve teaching salaries, and hire coaches. And when the teams are not performing well or not winning, the same board members are the recipients of telephone calls and newspaper editorials. Such complex informal communication networks necessitate knowing how to navigate through the maze of local politics and traditions. Constituency concerns, therefore, become critical to the effectiveness and survival of the administrator or educational leader.

The principal, superintendent, or other educational leader must be able to recognize the elements of the culture of the school and the role in which these elements play in the community. In effect, those in leadership positions become the gatekeepers of the school. Serving as guardians over the children of the community, the school administrator provides a safe and productive learning environment. Those in leadership positions are keepers of the school spirit, responsible for maintaining the spirit of unity and the sense of community within the experiences of the high school.

The high school principal also plays the leading role in maintaining the culture and traditions of the school, which have existed over the years. Changing or eliminating customs and/or traditions can be tricky and costly. The principal must recognize the value of each tradition and activity, weigh its merits against the mandates of the board and superintendent, make the appropriate decisions, and develop an effective plan of action. Recognizing the role and significance of the predominant athletic program, such as Bainesville football, providing and facilitating support for the program requires skill and insight—vision. The principal or superintendent must strategically postulate the importance of excelling academically in the classroom and athletically on the playing field.

The school leader and/or principal must play the role of gatekeeper. The high school principal must ensure that the school's traditions and rituals of value are maintained, communicated, and understood by the students, faculty, and staff as well as the members of the community. To complete this responsibility, the school leader must be able to recognize and understand the networking of the school culture. In small rural schools like Bainesville, understanding the role and impact of high school athletics on the school culture and the community becomes the standard by which they are evaluated.

Finally, the school leader or principal is the keeper of the school spirit. School spirit refers to the levels of enthusiasm and exuberance for the school, its athletic teams, its drama teams—everything that is symbolic of the school. The school leader's role is to ensure that a high level of enthusiasm and, thus, commitment is conveyed to the various members of the school community. The role as the keeper of the school spirit demands active participation and understanding of the school culture.

Cast in the arena of "systems of influence and control" (Goldring and Rallis 1993), principals and superintendents are seen as fitting neatly in a formal hierarchy, thus charged with the responsibilities of operating within the established boundaries of the structure of the organization—with the task of transforming, directing, and instructing as the operative constructs describing the action of the principal. In contrast, as described by Deal and Peterson (1994), the principal can shape a culture by participating in and encouraging the rituals that celebrate important values. Everyday tasks take on added significance when they symbolize values. School activities may become rituals when they express shared values and bind people in a common experience. When asked to describe her role as the principal of Bainesville High School and her mission or vision upon taking the job, Carla Jenette replied:

"My primary mission in taking this job was to restore pride and spirit back to this school and to this community. This school was a mess when I first visited with the superintendent. In fact, I turned down the first offer to take the job. I didn't turn it down because of money, but because the school was in such disarray. The superintendent called me several times over a two-month period, and I finally agreed to take the job. And I have had no regrets."

As principal of Bainesville High School, Jenette has worked diligently for three years toward restoring school pride, school spirit, and community pride toward the high school. She utilized a variety of strategies, techniques, and methods for achieving this goal. With her vision of a school full of students who are proud to call themselves Bainesville Indians, she set about her quest. She first hired a veteran football coach, known for his ability to build high school football teams and restore team pride—especially in situations where there are low expectations of pride, teamwork, or success. "Show me a high school without pride and success in its athletic teams, and I'll show you a school where there is no respect or school spirit or school pride. I think that the quality of the school's athletic teams and, more often than not, its football programs set the tone for both the school and the community," Jenette explained, sitting behind her desk with one arm crossed and the other arm propped under her chin, her eyebrows raised, exclaiming the intent of the seriousness of her comment.

Others apparently agreed with her philosophy, and this was echoed throughout the interviews. Jerry Daniels, a former supervisor with the Bainesville area parks and recreation department, made the following observation: "I think that organized sports and athletics in this community basically bring people together, and it fosters that community feeling. It [sports and athletics] gives the kids and parents' opportunities to get together, have a good time, and build relationships. With the new administration in the local school system, there has been a tremendous difference in the emphasis and attitude toward athletics at the school level, and that has had an impact at the park and recreational level."

School pride and school spirit can be found in other areas besides athletics. As Jenette made clear, her primary mission was to restore pride in the school. To ensure that parents and other community members were convinced and had a clear understanding that the objective was to make improvements for the high school as a whole, Jenette assumed the lead role as cheerleader, instructional leader, and community leader for the school.

"In taking this job, I knew we had to get back to the old traditions and, at the same time, introduce some new ones or at least a new spin for the old traditions," she explained. During the 1995–96 school year, the principal had designated a night for seniors and their parents. The event was organized as a "covered-dish" dinner where seniors and their parents received important information about graduation, financial aid for college, and the newly instituted senior picnic and senior trip.

For the grand finale, the seniors who were on track to graduate received specially designed shirts with their class motto printed on the front and a list of all the senior's names printed on the back. During the 1996–97 school year, as I attended the senior night event, the parents were outwardly appreciative of the efforts to provide information and communication. More apparent, however, was their appreciation for the recognition and emphasis placed on academic success and graduation.

This [senior night] makes us feel connected with the high school. Our kids don't always tell parents the things we need to know, like ordering invitations, meeting other graduation requirements . . . As a parent, I am very thankful for this. Just look around, the room is full of people . . . parents and their kids. It's just wonderful. (Parent of a senior)

The response from the seniors was also one of appreciation and acceptance. As I watched the interaction between Carla Jenette (the school principal) and her senior students, it became obvious that this was her night to demonstrate publicly that she cared for the students, the school, the parents, and the community.

"One of the highest forms of principal 'talk' is the story. A well-chosen story provides a powerful image . . . carries values and connects abstract ideas with emotions and events," wrote Deal and Peterson (1994) as they described the role of the principal. The importance of story and the images and feelings that are set in motion by the telling and retelling of past events and the importance placed on future participation is echoed by Bacharach and Mundell (1995, 112).

In every organized activity, it is important that people believe in what they are doing, share a common heritage and faith, and dream together. This provides meaning and spirit to fuel what they do with passion and purpose . . . It symbolically binds a people together . . . in a common quest.

The importance of academic success has been proclaimed as one of the major ingredients for building school pride. One teacher echoed that sentiment as she reflected on the role of athletics as compared to academics.

As one teacher reflected and recounted, "In the past, a lot of things were sacrificed for football. This has changed since the new administration. But in the past, football players and other well-known athletes weren't held to the same academic standard as the rest of the student body. I've had coaches . . . in the past . . . come to me and asked if I could give this athlete or that athlete a break on a test or some assignment that was due that week. And there happens to be a big game or something that week. It made me furious. But I must say, that has not happened since Ms. Jenette came and hired the new football coaches.

And indeed, the high school principal sets a high standard for behavior, attitude, and student responsibility. In discussing the academic side of her school, Ms. Jenette reflected: "In the past, this school has had a reputation of being weak on academics as well as sports. But there are some shining moments that are beginning to happen in this school. And it's exciting to me. For example, we had students who placed third in the region in literary meet just a few weeks ago, which we came in last place last year. We also had a student who placed fourth in the spelling bee for our region. And in the past, no one from this high school has participated. So all those types of activities that are of a competitive nature helps to build student pride, school spirit and reinforces the traditions of values and beliefs toward being strong academically. It's the little things that are important to individual students."

Her tireless promotion of hard work and school pride and of doing the right thing for students has solidified support from the community. In a discussion about the condition of the school's academics and athletics, one parent shared these thoughts: "The school [Bainesville High School] has seen a turnaround since Carla Jenette has been here. Before, our athletics were in terrible shape. We've had some bad experiences with some coaches in the past. Mrs. Jenette, by bringing in Coach Bill Mason, has added some stability there. She has been able to make some changes in the teaching staff, and that's been positive. Overall, I'd say that the school is in much better shape than it was three years ago. Also, several AP (advanced placement) courses have been added, and before [Mrs. Jenette], we didn't have any. So I'd say that we're in much better shape."

Another parent, whose child had attended other schools before entering the Bainesville system as a middle school student, said that Bainesville High School had a warm feeling about it.

"We moved up here from a larger more metropolitan-type school. There were more students at the other high school, and there seemed to be more problems with students and gangs and violence. Here [at Bainesville High School], there's seems to be more of a friendly atmosphere. I've met most of her [her child's] teachers, and I'm satisfied that the level of teaching is good. At least, I won't have to worry about my kid and whether or not she's safe," the parent said.

Then, Jenette set about cleaning up the campus. She recalled her first impressions; "There were three main goals I had when I took this job. I was determined to get the hats off the boys' heads (while in the building), I was determined to get the tobacco out of their mouths, and I was determined to get the food out of the hallways and bathrooms. I knew if I could accomplish those three things, I could restore some order and pride in this school," Said Jenette.

The principal promotes and believes that every parent and student should have a positive feeling about their school. The priorities that she has outlined support and reinforce the school system motto, which reads, Our Children Are Our Gold Mines. Her actions are grounded, she says, in the belief that all children should have as positive learning experiences as possible and that students (and faculty) should be involved in some aspect of the school.

"I know that if these kids are involved with some activity connected with this school, they will find a purpose and feel better about themselves and have pride in their school. If we can accomplish that, we've done a lot," Said Jenette.

As stated earlier, Jenette identified as one of her missions was the need to rebuild the pride and spirit in the school's football team. The football games, she noted, are major events in this community, a "family tradition for many who live here in this community," remarked Carla Jenette, principal of Bainesville High. The local newspaper, the *Bainesville Nuggett*, included in an early August edition a fall sports preview, featuring the Bainesville High School Indians. The six-page section of the newspaper contained pictures of athletes from all sports areas (e.g., football, baseball, track, girls' softball, soccer, basketball, and cheerleaders). It also contained stories about the students and coaches as well as messages from area businesses wishing the students and their teams' good luck for the coming season.

The school principal knows the value of participating in sports and the value of winning and losing. When asked to describe her background with sports and education, Jenette shared the following: "I have been in education for thirty-one years. I have worked at the junior high level, the high school level, and I have coached at both the high school and college levels. I have been an administrator for approximately twenty years now. I'm also married to a career coach; my husband has coached at both the high school and college levels also. So I have a long history with athletics."

One parent commented about the importance of athletics at Bainesville High School and the community, in support of the school principal's stance of strong athletic programs: "It's [athletics] running close to academics as far as importance and meaningfulness and contributions to the kids. I think it's very beneficial for those who participate. It provides a lot of school spirit. A lot of people [in the Bainesville community] like athletics and will go to the games. But to really get the fever going, you've got to have a winning program. I think that the new principal has certainly been a leader in that respect."

Still, another parent whose son had been involved in sports since beginning with the parks and recreation department, and now at the high school level expressed her support for athletics: "I think athletics are important because they help the teachers who teach academics. It's because you have another group of people keeping an eye on the kids and making sure they're performing. You've got somebody in-house [meaning the coaches] helping out. I think that [athletics and academics] are on an equal scale. You have to have one to have the other."

Henry Rhodes—parent, teacher, and community member—echoed the sentiment that seemed to surface throughout the interviews as people shared their views and opinions about the high school and its sports teams. When asked about high school athletics and the Bainesville community, he shared these thoughts:

"I think that athletics is such a vital part of the American culture, and I think the same thing is true for this community that some people in this community probably treat those who are athletes a little differently. Because the sacrifice that they make [the athletes], there should be some differences in treatment. They have to maintain their academics as well as play well on the field. Sport, in this community, has had an impact on the culture. I think that there should be something special for the kids who put I in the time and effort and commitment with practice and games. The schools have done a good job in keeping a balance."

The school has its share of critics. One community member and civic leader, when asked about his perceptions about the values and traditions of high school athletics in the Bainesville community, shared the following: "I think Bainesville has a significant attitude problem in that they work hard at trying not to lose. And I don't believe they have the understanding. It comes all the way from the table; and, when I say 'table,' I mean from the kitchen table. They have learned in many cases to accept losing."

When asked about the significance of high school sports to the community, the comments shifted to more support, reinforcing the role of high school athletics as important to the community and the school. "In the beginning of this season, I saw the stands full. Friday night football is the social event of the fall. Social interaction, look at our town. We don't have any nightclubs, we don't have any real fancy restaurants, we don't have any shopping centers, and we don't have anything else. So if you're going to interact with people, you go to one of the athletic events [of the high school]," he said.

Teachers and staff also concur with the notion that athletics play a major role in the school and community. Pete Summers, a veteran teacher and native Bainesvillian, expressed support and concern regarding the school's athletic program: "When I was in high school here, all we had were basketball and baseball . . . as far as competitive sports were concerned. In basketball, we won twenty or so games every year. We went to region most every year. The school was the focal point of the community. I think that it [the school] still is the main focal point for this community. But I think what has happened is that there's too much going on. In the school year now, at any given time, there are three sports going on at the same time. We're too spread out."

Athletics, especially in small towns and rural communities, represent tradition and homespun values of family, discipline, and perseverance. As the high school principal, Carla Jenette described her approach toward athletics, "You keep the very best of traditions and what people feel are important in place, yet insert a "new spin" occasionally to make them more interesting or to get more people involved. It's important for each student to enjoy each act individually—each tradition. But there are some things that are old traditions and should be held in place. They're important for the school, the students, and the community. Take the school alma mater. The kids and faculty didn't know it. Those things are old traditions that shouldn't die. They're rallying cries and provide a special feeling of belonging. Things like the school song, the mascot, the school colors, and the flag . . . are all identifiers of the school and reinforce the meaning of the old traditions," she said.

I asked Jenette to describe two new traditions that have been enacted since she has been principal. With a deep breath and a chuckle, the she said, "I have two good ones to tell you about." "This year, I took it upon myself to order a purple flag with an Indian embroidered in gold on it. None of the kids, except for two or three, knew about the flag. It measures six feet by eight feet. We unveiled it at the homecoming game pep rally, and the kids just loved it. It was the greatest thing. The new flag became the new symbol to help reinforce the school spirit. Letter jackets to football players or athletes who letter in two sports were bought by booster club. Rebuilding the spirit has been a major objective, trying to get back to the old traditions," she said.

"The second new tradition we have started has to do with the awarding of a letter jacket to an athlete when he or she has earned two or more letters in their given sports. One of the tasks that I asked the head coach to do was to completely revamp the criteria for earning a letter. To me, it has to mean something. And the letter jackets must mean something too. It's all part of building pride. Well, this year we will have two non-senior athletes who will have earned at least two athletic letters. The booster club has agreed to purchase the jackets, and they're all leather—no cheapies. We have to do this first class. It's all part of building pride . . . weaving the old traditions with the new traditions to build school spirit," she recounted.

Conclusion

Studying the relationship between the Bainesville Indian's football program, the high school culture, and the connections with the community has offered a unique look into the complexities of everyday life at Bainesville High School and at the mission and passion for traditions and values sought by the school principal. Certainly, to replicate this study in another small rural community would strengthen and give credence to the validity of the study. Further research and replication, an expansion of this study, would provide significant insight into the complex world of rural America. Further study will, perhaps, facilitate the development of potential solutions for providing quality educational opportunities in under funded rural high schools while allowing them to protect and defend their highly coveted way of life.

Still, another consideration deals with the aspect of high school sports and athletics. Further research into the significance of high school athletics in rural settings would clarify its role in the total high school experience as well as contribute to the understanding of its role in the development of the community and the community sports culture. High school sports in small rural areas are major entities within the community, connected and reinforced by the strings and ties of emotion and memory.

Further research and study of rural communities and of what makes these communities special places to live will only add to the overall understanding of American culture. As Alan Peshkin (1978, 88) noted in his study of the rural community of Mansfield, those whom he interviewed referred to their way of life as "the way we do things around here." On any given Friday night when the Bainesville High Indians are playing football under the bright lights of the stadium, with the band playing and the crowd cheering with their painted golden jugs raised mightily in the air, it is simply "the way we do things around here."

The End! . . . Finally . . . Perhaps?

Chapter Fifteen

Update from Bainesville

At the time of the writing of this chapter, it has been a decade since I left the school I referred to as "Bainesville." I moved on to work as a high school principal for a few years and later as a superintendent. The lessons gleaned from my research and experiences, in my view, still hold true today. No matter how many school reforms are enacted, no matter what Nuevo Professional Learning Communities are seen as the new silver bullet for better schools, in order to be successful in the process of teaching and learning, whether you are an administrator or a teacher, you must know the culture of your school and community, and you must have a passion for kids, whatever the age. Teaching and learning is as much an "Art" as it is a "Science." A friend who is also a teacher and aspiring administrator recounted a comment overheard from one of his school administrators, that there wasn't time for "teachable moments, that teachers had to teach the standards." My strong advice and recommendation for anyone, be it a teacher or administrator, is that you never, and I do mean NEVER, lose sight of the reason you get up every morning and stand before a classroom filled with students. Don't become blinded by all the political rhetoric and whims of the day, such that it sucks from you your love and passion for teaching. Never forget what it looks like and feels like to see a child's eyes light up when that "moment of learning" occurs, when that student "gets it!"

****

Fourteen years have passed since the case study research was done, and athletics in Bainesville continue to break new ground. Carla Jenette, the principal charged with the task of renewing the traditions and culture of the high school has since retired. Bainesville High School now has had several new football coaches, has gone to the regional and state play-offs for the first time in the history of the school and football program, and now has a new high school and new stadium.

In recent years, the entire town closed down, as the student body, parents, teachers, and community folks lined the street coming from the high school leading out of town toward the team's destination—their next foe. Children and their parents and grandparents lined the side of the road, all waving flags or streamers of purple and gold; a kind of "Blessing of the Team" as they passed by, as if to say, "Go forth young men and women, and represent us well." It was magical!

The old stadium, A. P. King Field, stands quiet like a ghostly battlefield, absent of conflict and the smell that accompanies cool brisk air, sweat, and the congregation of hundreds of faithful fans. The concrete bleachers that look out over the Blue Ridge Mountains seem deserted, almost dejected, as if abandoned by a family whose roots run deep and span several decades. The grass on the football field is uncut and absent of foot traffic as the tall sponsor board that stands at the southeast end of the field just beyond the end zone keeps vigil over the stadium.

There have been several changes in personnel at Bainesville High School. In addition to the new football coach, two other coaches have also left the school. One moved to another town and is coaching for another high school while another moved to Mississippi, leaving the teaching and coaching profession altogether. Two assistant principals have retired; and I, as the other assistant principal, have moved on to another school, taking the reins as high school principal. But there have been some sad losses, as well.

Bainesville High School was like an extended family. And, as with most families, the passing of a close family member tends to bring you closer together and tends to make you stronger as a collective group, if only for a short time. There have been three losses in the Bainesville family. One was an English teacher with whom I shared a teaching unit and a love for William Faulkner, whom we both admired and often discussed at lunch.

She was truly loved and admired, respected and revered, which was illustrated by the reading of a letter by one of her former students at the chapel service during her funeral. "She made me believe in myself because she believed in me and told me so every day. I'm a better person because of her," the student read as tears ran down his cheeks. The chapel was mournfully quiet except for the sniffles, and the audience cried silently with the young man pouring his heart out, reading from his soul. The year before, the students dedicated the yearbook to her as their tribute to a true teacher of life as well as academics. The cancer that had encroached upon her body in the summer and fall took her life in early spring. After months of chemotherapy and harsh drugs, she chose her path. She died quietly with her two sons beside her bed at home. She is missed.

Bainesville's second loss came in the early fall of 2001. This person was a paraprofessional and a supporter of the Bainesville High Indians for many years. She attended every home game of every sport for ten years or more. She was the person you met upon entering the gate at the old stadium, sitting at a table, taking money and ushering in fans and friends at home basketball games, or arriving early at baseball and softball games. But more than that, she was a friend. She raised three children as a single parent and taught them the value of hard work, honesty, humility, and, most of all, love—love of family and of friends. She loved kids. Her life revolved around her kids and the school. And as her own kids grew older and went on to college or to work as young adults, she adopted the students at school as her second family of kids.

The memorial service was a reflection of her love for nature, love for Bainesville, and love for kids, especially those who might be having a hard time coping with life. She had just accepted a job, her first new job in over ten years, as a camp counselor and camp supervisor at a local summer camp for children. Her memorial service was held at the chapel of the camp, surrounded by nature with a waterfall and mountain laurel as a backdrop for the many songs played and sung in her honor. She had planned out her last rites. She wanted to be surrounded by trees and nature and family and friends. She also touched many lives and is truly missed.

The third person who is no longer with us attended as well as taught at Bainesville High School. She was loved and adored by parents, students, and staff. She was a dedicated and faithful member of the Bainesville community. Her presence in the halls of the vocational wing at the high school is sorely missed.

The new school is beautifully designed and provides visitors with a majestic welcome much like the gateway to the Great Smoky Mountains. The students who were a part of the story of Bainesville have graduated and either married, gone to college or have chosen their careers. From time to time, whenever I am at a football or basketball game, I'll see familiar faces. We'll embrace and share stories as we all provide updates to each other about life and family. Similar to a family reunion, only smaller in scale, we sit, gathered on several bleacher seats, intensely engaged in conversation while the game and all its noise and history-making unfold in the background. And then, the buzzer sounds, the game is over. We hug and say good-bye. The Bainesville High family has once again been reinforced.

All the rituals, celebrations, and ceremonies that I studied and researched that eventually produced my dissertation, are the basis for this book and are all celebrated in full fashion. The crowds still gather on Friday nights, and some still meet early to tailgate in the parking lot outside the new football stadium. Those golden jugs filled with rocks still sound the call for the crowd to stand and cheer. Welcome to Bainesville, home of the Indians!

Chapter Sixteen

Thoughts and Reflections

I began the journey of collecting data in preparation for writing a dissertation in the fall of 1996. Three years later, after many revisions and the help and guidance of my dissertation advisor, I graduated. The ceremony of graduation at Vanderbilt University was awe inspiring. I savored every moment. After the main ceremony near the tower in the center of the Vanderbilt campus, the various schools were dismissed to their respective campuses. I made my way to Peabody College, just across the campus on the other side of Twenty-First

Street. I had arranged for my family to meet there since the south side of Nashville was teeming with parents, grandparents, and various other family and friends who were in attendance this graduation weekend. The Peabody ceremony was nothing less than first class, complete with a five-piece orchestral ensemble that played continuously during the reception underneath the large tent where graduates, their families, and alumni gathered around the hors d'oeuvres and wine decanters.

The last stop was in the basement of the Social Science building which had recently been renovated and restored to resemble the center of academia in Gothic Rome. It was in this small room that the graduation regalia was either returned or purchased. This, I decided, was an appropriate purchase. After all, I had earned it. So when it was my turn and the young lady asked if I was returning or purchasing, I said gladly, "I'm purchasing; how much?"

"Three hundred fifty dollars," she replied. "Will that be cash, check, or credit card?"

With sweat beading on my forehead, I reached for my wallet, pulled out my Visa Card, and made my purchase. Still feeling a bit numb from the ceremony, exhausted from the whole experience, I made my way outside to my waiting family. My wife also asked how much to which I quickly replied, "You don't want to know, but after all this, it's worth it!"

The journey of education from my bachelor's degree, which took eight years to complete, to my doctor of education degree had been a long and arduous one, with many sacrifices having been required as fare. The experience at Vanderbilt, especially Peabody College, yielded many life lessons and created many close friends as well. I have always been intrigued by people and why they do what they do, and what motivates them. This led to an insatiable interest in the aspects of leadership and organizational culture.

I could never have imagined or predicted the depth of the Peabody experience. It truly has had a major impact on my life, both personally and professionally; I'm glad that part of my life's journey is completed. As viewed from a lifetime of learning, however, the Peabody experience as a doctoral student was only the opening of the door.

References

Anderson, C., R. Fisher, S. C. Jones, B. Peterson, and C. R. Ramsay. 1974. *Life in rural America*. Washington, DC: National Geographic Society.

Argus. 1971. Bainesville, GA: Bainesville High School.

Argus. 1990. Bainesville, GA: Bainesville High School.

Bacharach, S., and B. Mundell. 1995. *Images of schools: Structures and rules in organizational behavior.* Thousand Oaks, CA: Corwin Press.

Barker, B. O. 1986. *The advantages of small schools.* Las Cruces, StNM: ERIC Clearinghouse on Rural Education and Small Schools.

Beck, L., and J. Murphy. 1996. *The four imperatives of a successful school*. Thousand Oaks, CA: Corwin Press.

Bellah, R. 1985. *Habits of the heart*. Berkeley, CA: Univ. of California Press.

Berry, W. 1977. *The unsettling of America: Culture and agriculture*. San Francisco, CA: Sierra Club Books.

Bissinger, H. G. (1991). *Friday night lights: A town, a team, and a dream*. New York: Harper Perennial Press.

Bingman, M. B., and C. White. 1994. Appalachian communities: Working to survive. *Alpha 94: Literacy and Cultural Development Strategies in Rural Areas*. Education Retrieval Document No. ED 386 356.

Bobbett, G. C., et al. 1990. A study of six Appalachian high schools. Paper presented at the annual meeting of the Mid-South Educational Research Association. Appalachia Educational Labs., Charleston, WV. ERIC Document Reproduction Service No. ED 326 559.

Bobbett, G. C., and others. 1991. A study of "goodness" in six rural Appalachian high schools. Paper presented at the annual meeting of the American Educational Research Association. Appalachia Educational Labs., Charleston, WV. ERIC Document Reproduction Service No. ED 339 559.

Bolman, L. G., and T. E. Deal. 1991. *Reframing Organizations: Artistry, choice, and leadership.* San Francisco, CA: Jossey-Bass.

Boyer, E. 1995. *The basic school: A community for learning.* Princeton, NJ: The Carnegie Foundation.

Bryant, M. T., and M. L. Grady. 1990. Community factors threatening rural school district stability. Journal of Research in Rural Education, 6 (3): 21–26.

Bryk, A., and M. Driscoll. 1988. *The high school as community: Contextual influences and consequences for students and teachers.* Madison, WI: Wisconsin Center for Educational Research, Univ. of Wisconsin–Madison.

Calhoun, D. W. 1987. *Sport, culture, and personality.* Champaign, IL: Human Kinetics Publishers, Inc.

Colfer, A. M., and C. J. P. Colfer. 1979. Life and learning in an American town: Quilcene, WA: National Institute of Education, Washington, DC. ERIC Document Reproduction Service No. ED 201 444.

Coleman, J. S. 1988. Social capital in the creation of human capital. *Journal of Sociology* 94, Supplement: S95-S120.

Coles, R. 1993. *The call of service: A witness to idealism* New York: Houghton Mifflin Company.

Conway, G. 1994. Small scale and school culture: The experience of private schools. N.p.: ERIC Clearinghouse on Rural Education and Small Schools. ERIC Document Reproduction Service No. ED 376 996.

Cox, H. 1969. *The Feast of fools*. Cambridge, MA: Harvard Univ. Press.

Cromatie, R. L. 1994. *Auburn vs. Alabama, Braggin' rights*. Atlanta, GA: Gridiron Publishers.

Crowson, R., and W. Boyd. 1993. Coordinating services for children: Designing arks for storms and seas unknown. *American Journal of Education* 101 (2): 140–179.

Crowson, R. L. 1992. *School-community relations, under reform*. Berkeley, CA: McCutchan Publishing Corporation.

Deal, T. E. 1993. The culture of schools. M. Sashkin and Walberg, eds., *Educational leadership and school culture*, 3–15. National Society for the Education Publication.

Deal, T. 1995. Symbols and symbolic activity. Bacharach and Mundell, *Images of schools*, 108–136. Thousand Oaks, CA: Corwin Press.

Deal, T., and S. Nutt. 1979. Planned change in rural school districts. Baldridge and Deal, *The dynamics of organizational change in education*. Berkeley, CA.: McCutchan Publishing Corporation.

Deal, T. E., and K. D. Peterson. 1994. *The leadership paradox: Balancing logic and artistry in schools.* San Francisco, CA: Jossey-Bass.

Deavers, K. L., and D. L. Brown. 1985. Natural resource dependence, rural development, and rural poverty. Rural Development   Research Report No. 48. Economic Research Service, Washington, DC, ED 258 775.

Denlinger, K. 1994. *For the glory: College football dreams and realities inside Paterno's program.* New York, NY: St. Martin's Griffen Press.

DeYoung, A. J. 1989. *Economics and American education.* New York, NY: Longman Press.

DeYoung, A. J. 1991. *Struggling with their histories: Economic decline and educational improvement in four rural southeastern school districts.* Norwood, NJ: Ablex Publishing Corporation.

Driver, T. F. 1991. *The magic of ritual: Our need for liberating rites that transform our lives and our communities.* San Francisco, CA: Harper Collins Press.

Dunne, F. 1981. Is there such a thing as rural education? A portrait of the small rural school. *The Small School Forum* 2: 2–4.

Durkheim, E. 1984. *The division of labor in society.* Trans. W. D. Halls. The Free Press. (Original work published in 1893).

Etizioni, A. 1993. *The spirit of community: The reinvention of American society.* New York: Simon & Schuster.

Friedman, M. 1982. Feminism and modern friendship: Dislocating the community. C. Sunstein, ed., *Feminism and political theory,* 143–158. Chicago: Univ. of Chicago Press.

Fulghum, R. 1995. *From beginning to end: Rituals of our lives.* New York: Ivy Books.

Fuller, W. E. 1982. *The old country school.* Chicago, IL: Univ. of Chicago Press.

Furtwengler, W. J., and A. Micich. 1991. Seeing what we think: Symbols of school culture. Chicago, IL: American Educational Research Association. ERIC Documentation Reproduction Service No. ED 335 754.

Galbraith, M. W. 1992. *Education in the rural American community.* Malabar, FL: Krieger Publishing Company.

Geertz, C. 1973. *The interpretation of cultures.* New York: Basic Books.

Goldring, E., and S. Rallis. 1993. *Principals of dynamic schools.* Newbury Park, CA: Corwin Press.

Goodlad, J. 1984. *A place called school: Prospects for the future.* New York: McGraw-Hill Book Company.

— — —. 1997. County Community Overview. Atlanta, GA: Georgia Department of Labor.

Gordon, D. 1992. The symbolic dimension of administration for effective schools. San Francisco, CA: American Educational Research Association. ERIC Document Reproduction Service No. ED 349 659.

Grant, G. 1988. *The world we created at Hamilton High*. Cambridge, MA: Harvard Univ. Press.

Hargreaves, J. 1986. *Sport, power and culture*. Oxford, ENG: Polity Press.

Hobbs, D. 1988. *Community economic development innovation: The key to rural school improvement and rural vitalization*. Kansas City, MO: Mid-Continent Regional Educational Laboratory.

Horrigan, K. 1992. *The right kind of heroes*. San Francisco, CA: HarperCollins Publishers.

Jonassen, C. T. 1968. *Community conflict in school district reorganization*. Oslo, NOR: Universitetsforlaget.

Killian, L. 1977. Minimize or maximize? Education and training for tomorrow's technical Navy. Paper presented at the annual meeting of the Association of Educational Communications and Technology. Miami Beach, FL.

Kirk, W. D., and S. Kirk. 1993. Student athletes: Shattering the myths and sharing the realities. American Counseling Association. Alexandria, VA. ERIC Document Reproduction Service No. ED 348 583.

Kohlenberg, E., and D. Kohlenberg. 1991. *Human services in small towns and rural areas: Linking distant providers with community care systems.* Seattle, WA: Northwest Policy Center.

Kozol, J. 1991. *Savage inequalities: Children in America's schools.* New York: Harper Perennial Press.

LeCompte, M. D., and J. Preissle. 1993. *Ethnography and qualitative design in educational research.* 2nd ed. San Diego, CA: Academic Press.

Lincoln, Y. S., and E. G. Guba. 1985. *Naturalistic inquiry.* Newbury Park, CA: SAGE Publications.

Luschen, G. R. F., and G. H. Sage. 1981. *Handbook of social science of sport.* Champaign, IL: Stipes Publishing Company.

Madsen, R., W. M. Sullivan, and R. N. Bellah. 1992. *The good society.* New York: Vintage Books.

Martinez, L. P. 1989. Principal as artist: A model for transforming a school community. Doctoral Dissertation, Peabody College at Vanderbilt Univ., 1989.

Merz, C., and G. Furman. 1997. *Community and schools: Promise and paradox.* New York: Teachers College Press, Columbia Univ.

Miles M. B., and A. M. Huberman. 1994. Qualitative Data Analysis. 2nd ed. Thousand Oaks, CA: SAGE Publications.

Miller, B. A. 1991. *Distress and survival: Rural schools, education, and the importance of community.* Portland, OR: Regional Educational Laboratory.

— — —. 1995. The role of rural schools in rural community development. Clearinghouse on Rural Education and Small Schools. Charleston, WV: Appalachia Educational Laboratory.

Miller, B. 1993. *Promising rural practices in school-to-work transition: Portrait one, Broadus, Montana.* Portland, OR: Northwest Regional Educational Laboratory.

Moore, S. F., and B. G. Myerhoff. 1977. *Secular ritual.* Assen/Amsterdam, NETH: Van Gorcum.

Nachtigal, P. 1989. What's noteworthy on rural schools and community development. Mid-Regional Educational Laboratory. Office of Educational Research and Improvement, Washington, DC, Mid-Continent Regional Educational Laboratory. ERIC Document Reproduction Service No. ED 313 177.

— — —. 1997. School-community survey. National Study of School Evaluation. Schaumburg, IL.

Nettles, S. M. 1992. Coaching in community settings. Center on Families, Communities, Schools, and Children's Learning. John Hopkins Univ., Baltimore, MD. ERIC Document Reproduction Service No. ED 346 083.

O'Hare, W. 1988. The rise of poverty in rural America. Washington, DC: Population Referendum Bureau. ERIC Document Reproduction Service No. ED 302 350.

O'Toole. J. 1995. *Leading change: Overcoming the ideology of comfort and tyranny of custom.* San Francisco, CA: Jossey-Bass.

Owen, H. 1987. *Spirit: Transformation and development in organizations.* Potomac, MD: Abbott Publishing.

Peshkin, A. 1978. *Growing up American: Schooling and the survival of community.* Chicago, IL: The Univ. of Chicago Press.

Peshkin, A. 1993. The goodness of qualitative research. *Educational Researcher* 22 (2): 24–30.

Porter, K. 1989. Poverty in rural America: A national overview. Washington, DC: Center on Budget Policy and Priorities. ERIC Document Reproduction Service No. ED 309 901.

Putnam, R. 1995. Bowling alone: America's declining social capital. *Journal of Democracy* 6 (1): 65–78.

Redfield, R. 1941. *The folk culture of the Yucatan.* Chicago, IL: Univ. of Chicago Press.

Redfield, R. 1950. *A village that chose progress.* Chicago, IL: Univ. of Chicago Press.

Reid, J. 1990. Education and rural development: A review of recent evidence. Paper presented at the annual meeting of the American Educational Research Association, Boston, MA.

Roberts, D. February 1995. Dixie living: Southern people. Southern style: Rolling with the tide. One game writer's adventures on the road with the pride of Alabama. *Atlanta Journal-Constitution*. N.p.

Roberts, D. December, 1998. 50,000 fans can't be wrong. *The Oxford American*. 23: 32–36.

Ryan, V. D. 1987. Rural economic development in the 1980s: Preparing for the future. Economic Research Service. Washington, DC. ED 313 211.

Schien, E. 1992. *Organizational cultures and leadership*. 2nd ed. San Francisco, CA: Jossey-Bass.

Schmuck, R. A., and P. A. Schmuck. 1989. Democratic participation in small-town schools. Unpublished manuscript. Univ. of Oregon, Eugene, Oregon & Lewis and Clark College, Portland, OR.

Schmuck, P. 1992. The lessons of school restructuring: The advantage of being a small school district. Paper presented to the annual convention of the National Rural Education Association. ERIC Document Reproduction Service No. ED 355 074.

Sher, J. P. 1977. *Education in rural America: A reassessment of conventional wisdom*. Boulder, CO: Westview Press.

Siddle-Walker, E. 1993. Caswell training school, 1933–1969: Relationships between community and schools. *Harvard Educational Review*, 6 (2): 161–185.

Shankin, B. 1994. *Against all odds*. New York, NY: Barclay House.

Shapiro, I. 1989. Laboring for less: Working but poor in rural America. Washington, DC: Center on Budget and Policy Priorities. ERIC Document Reproduction Service No. ED 319 566.

Smrekar, C. 1996. *The impact of school choice and community: In the interest of families and schools.* Albany, NY: State Univ. of New York Press.

Stake, R. E. 1975. *Evaluating the arts in education: A responsive approach.* Columbus, OH: Charles E. Merrill.

Tonnies, F. 1957. *Community and society.* Trans. and ed., Charles Loomis. East Lansing, MI: Michigan State Univ. Press. (Original work published as *Gemeinschaft and Gesellschaft*, 1887).

Toqueville, A. 1945. *Democracy in America.* Trans., H. Reeves. Ed., P. Bradley. New York: Vintage Books. (Original work published 1835).

Tuckman, B. W. 1988. *Conducting educational research.* 3rd ed. San Diego, CA: Harcourt Brace Jovanovich Publishers.

Versteeg, D. 1993. The rural high school as community resource. Educational Leadership, 54–55.

Wiebusch, J., and B. Silverman. 1994. *A game of passion.* Atlanta, GA: Turner Publishing Company.

Yin, R. K. 1994. *Case study research: Design and methods.* 2nd ed. Applied Social Research Methods Series, 5. Thousand Oaks, CA: SAGE Publications.

Coming Soon!

The next new novel by

Jesse R. Hale

Enjoy this introductory sample of

the first few chapters.

~ Football Town ~

Island Castaways

A Story of Adventure, Intrigue, and a Dead Body

A Novel

By Jesse R. Hale

*Published by Shades Creek Press, LLC
Savannah, Georgia, 2011.*

Chapter One

The dew still glistened on the leaves of the trees planted along the street-side, and only a few people dotted the sidewalks and art galleries, as I sat down with a large mocha java and a copy of the Asheville Times, when Carl walked up and asked the question he had been longing to corner me on. It was Sunday morning here in the mountains of North Carolina, in this hidden jewel of a city, where it really had become a melting pot of cultures and life styles. This had been the city where would we come as often as we could to escape the pressures of the daily grind, the work-a-day world of traffic, egos, and cigarette smoke, with countless nameless faces of people who were unfriendly either out of fear or their own smugness.

Alas, here I sat, finally back in the Eden of the mountainous world of free America, where free-thinking and openness was expected virtues and characteristics of those who resided or visited this city.   And this coffee shop was a great little hideaway, an escape from most. "So, Ethan," Carl said, as he approached, wiping a table or two in the way over to may table; "Tell me what happened? I've been dying to know the details."   Carl sat down with me at the small table outside his coffee café'.

We had arrived back in Atlanta at Hartsfield-Jackson International Airport, and promptly rented a car and drove straight through to Asheville, to our townhouse near the Grove Park Inn.   It was so relaxing; it was like stepping into the most luxurious spa in the world, like the Grove Park Inn was originally, back in the 1920's and 30's.   There was finally a sense of peace and relaxation, and safety. We could finally breathe.

"Where's Julie?" Carl asked, almost without taking a breath. Carl had been a close friend and confidant of ours since our college days. He had finished his MBA at Kennesaw State, and headed for the mountains. Ten years later, and after waiting tables and tending bar, Carl had scraped together enough money to open his dream business, a small coffee & book café'. With a modest yearly membership fee of fifty dollars, one can have access to books, DVDs, and the internet along with the newly installed SKYP for person-to-person communication. We had seen a lot of this type technology in Belize, and other parts of Central America where we had traveled.

"She's out shopping," I said, folding my paper. Carl was as eager as a kid being sent to bed on Christmas Eve to wait for the arrival of Saint Nick and Rudolph. "So, tell me, would you do it again?"

"Well, Carl, it started like this. It was an incredible trip, and yes, I'd do it again, but believe me, having gone through what we went through, we would do it much differently," I said, folding the paper and taking a sip of my coffee. I began the recounting of this tale.

It began with my waking up on the beach with sand and sea water in my mouth. The voyage over from Galveston Bay had been great, and a real blast, but it should have been a clue as to what lie ahead. "You know, Carl, we probably will have to finish this up over dinner and a bottle of good Pinot Giorgio, but here goes..."

"The ride on the windjammer from Galveston Bay was touted to be the best ride in that part of the Gulf, and it wasn't too expensive. We had worked out our schedule and were to meet the others on Ambergris Caye off the coast of Belize. But, nobody knew what would come when darkness engulfed the voyage. Man, was it strange. I still don't know some of the pieces of what happened.

I'm just glad it worked out; we were really lucky," I said as I began to tell the story of our strange adventure to the Central American coast of Belize, and the small island town of San Pedro.

Things took a bizarre turn when I found myself stranded on the beach, not knowing where the hell I was, or how I got there, and then Julie was missing. I had no memory of what had happened, at least not at first.

Carl issued orders to the two students who had arrived for their shift at the coffee café, and as Carl sat with both elbows on the table, his chin resting in his cupped hands with eager eyes for the rest of the story, I began a conversation that would indeed require several bottles of wine over dinner.

***　　　***　　　***　　　***

The water washed around me, retreating with the rhythm of waves crashing, as the sun broke the darkness and the morning sounds of seagulls and motorboats could be heard in the distance. A misty fog lay over the bay and the damp salty air served as a reminder of the crashing waves and hollowing winds of the ocean storm the night before. I lay there suddenly feeling every sharp edge of every grain of sand, imagining that it was caked so thick over my body that the sense of dread was overwhelming. Then, gasping suddenly; I realized that I had a gritty taste of sand in my mouth. It was incredibly salty and foreign. I had been laying face-down on the beach all night, but now, the sun was burning down on me. Every bone in my body ached, and my head ached, and I felt as if I had been kicked by a mule. Where was Julie, I wondered, then realizing the shock of my predicament, I began to muster the strength to pull myself up from the sand. I thought I knew at that point what had happened, but not really; it was all a blur.

The ocean water rushed over my feet as I stumbled to stand and walk down the beach; panic struck. Julie was missing! What had happened?

Where was she, and how the hell did I get into this situation? I couldn't concentrate on anything else; where was Julie; the question burned in my mind. I yelled, "Julie, Julie, where are you?" Again and again, "Where are you?" I would scream. It was surreal, like a science fiction movie, only I was playing the starring role, right there, on the beach. Stunned is an understatement.

***　　　　***　　　　***

As I retold the story and recounted the details of the trip, I considered how the trip and the experience had changed me, and us. It was nothing like we had expected or planned. It was more. Carl was a close friend, and I wasn't sure if I could convey the full impact the experiences had had on Julie and me.

On the beach that morning, as scared and shook as I was, I fell to my knees, losing control of my emotions, and cried for a while, with my face buried in my hands. I pulled myself up from the surf, stood stiff and tense, although bewildered and confused with the details of the night before being a bit fuzzy, I just stood there, and was speechless. The waves were almost knocking me over.

The sun was very bright and hot, such that occurs between the morning hours of 8:00 and 10:00, just when it starts heating up. The intensity of the heat from the bright sunshine was incredible; sweat was already dripping from his forehead, mixing with the sand and sea water dried on his face from lying on the beach all night. My head was aching, one of those migraine-type headaches that I sometimes got, and my eyelids were now beginning to be a part of that ache.

"What the heck happened?" I mumbled, looking in first one direction, then the other, trying to figure out not only what had happened, but where I was, and more desperately, where was Julie? With all the strength I could muster, I suppressed over my fear and panic, but finally giving in, I screamed, "Dang-it! Where is Julie?"

Feeling overwhelmed by the panic, I found the shade of some palm trees, sat down, and began to gather my thoughts, to let my analytical mind do its sorting. It was the kind of thing I was known for. I had made a lot of money playing the role of "problem solver" for corporations and non-profits, working first with consulting companies, and eventually moving out on my own, freelancing in the business of making people in highly competitive fast-paced jobs feel gratified and secure with their jobs and their workplace. Now, I was faced with the greatest challenge, my life.

The hunger in my stomach broke the concentration, realizing that I had not eaten since the party aboard the ship, two days after we had sailed from Galveston Bay. The reconstruction of my memory and the details of events during the last 24 hours were falling into place. The boat ride had been long and grueling, filled with craziness beyond belief. Two people had fallen overboard, or had they been pushed? This thought had been in my head, but no one had seemed concerned. Was I delirious, or was there something too crazy and insane to believe this was happening?

Standing up slowly, every muscle and bone aching' I gazed around trying to decide which direction to begin my course. I remembered that the ship had set a course southeast, and then southwest, toward the northern quarter of Belize, sailing approximately 85 miles around and south of the Yucatan Peninsula. "Well now, Oh Captain, My Captain, I think I'll face east and turn south." I mumbled; feeling a bit more confident, and a heck of a lot less panicky. I kept thinking positive thoughts about Julie, the love of my life. Perhaps she was up ahead. "I'll find her, I know it; I just know it," I mumbled to myself as I began walking up the beach, silently. Then, I prayed... *"Dear God, give me the strength to endure, and please keep Julie safe. Amen."* I looked toward the sky, as if asking God directly. Tears filled my eyes.

After walking for what seemed hours, I looked at the sun and calculated it to be about 12:00 Noon, remembering the position of the sun when I began walking.

"If I'm guessing right, and if I am where I think I am, San Pedro should be somewhere up ahead, unless I have landed off the coast of southern Mexico, which was my hope against hope, for that would be an almost impossible situation, almost as hostile of some parts of Guatemala," thinking out loud to myself. Jerry, my brother-in-law, and I had sailed around the island of Ambergris Caye, north of the mainland of Belize, on a previous trip. I could only hope that's where I was now. If so, then perhaps I could find Julie and the others, and figure out what had happened the night before on the ship to land me on the beach passed out all night. It wasn't my habit to drink to the point that I would pass out and not remember a thing. Rather, I suspected that something more sinister was at play, and I hoped that Julie was safe. My mood had now moved from panic and fear, to that of being ticked off and mad as a wet hen, as my mother used to say. But I knew I had to keep my cool and stay focused.

Chapter Two

Stopping underneath the shade of some palm trees, exhausted and sunburned from the heat rays that fell directly on the back of my neck, and my feet burning from the sand, using my left hand to block the sun, I looked to the south and realized my luck was about to change, "I'll just be doggone! Land Ho!"   My lips were parched and I was thirsty beyond imagination.

Gathering my wits, I began walking again. As I slid my feet through the hot sand, I thought about trying not to look too obvious.   Within a few minutes, I reached the outskirts of San Pedro, the village located on the north end of the island.

"Right!" I thought, as I analyzed the situation, and thought about the probable co-ordinances from the ship, my mind kicked in gear, "I can just imagine someone asking, 'where had I been and why was I dressed like that?'" My mind wandered further, "Oh, pardon me, Sir," I thought (mimicking a thick English accent), "but I have just arrived at this enchanted island paradise by way of floating like a dead person; darn cheap way to travel, I must say." "Right again," Shaking my head, and feeling even more confident, but a little stupid.

In the distance, I could see a long pier that extended far into the gulf. I knew that it was a public dock. As I got closer, I could faintly see people standing all along the length of the pier, fishing.

"That's a good sign. People are fishing. I must be close to the village somewhere ahead, and I hope it is San Pedro." As I thought about the prospects of having washed up on Ambergris Cay, after some mysterious and bizarre events still locked in the fog of my mind, I grew excited about the possibilities of finding Julie. Seeing people on the pier had given me a fresh breath of air and of energy, similar to having reached a trail head at a peak after hiking up the Appalachian Trail some 3000 feet. I felt exhilarated. My gait became more brisk and more determined, and before long I had arrived at the steps near the pier, steps which led to the village. Pausing to catch my breath, I tried to take in the scenes around me, turning from right to left, trying to notice every detail, trying the remember the way in which the town of San Pedro had looked. But it had been years since the last trip down and we had stayed on the south end of the island, and more importantly and even more significantly, Belize and Ambergris Cay had been discovered. It had changed. It had been, for years, a well-known secret dive spot for divers and adventurers, but had avoided the transformations and trappings of commercialism and the resort barrage. But my mind was on finding Julie. And, at this point, whether I was lucky enough to have washed up on Ambergris Cay or not, I somehow did not feel threatened. I felt determined.

"Let's go, mate," I again said aloud, as if I had a traveling companion. At the top of the steps I stopped, looked long and surveyed slowly and deliberately, and in the distance I heard voices and laughter coming from the sidewalk cafes and bars, and from people walking in and out of the small shops. "What about Julie," I thought, "where was she? What happened to her?" My mind drifted from panicky thoughts to the feeling of damn the torpedoes, to the reality that I still wasn't sure what had happened, or whether danger still lurked around the next corner. I had to keen and attentive.

Looking disheveled with my clothes torn and stained, and dried from the ocean air, I walked toward the voices and the laughter. The gravel on the street was like a fine dust, easy on my feet, which felt good. I was bare-footed and the sun-warmed powder felt good and encouraging; my feet still felt numb; the crushed rocks was a strange pleasure at a strange time. Turning the corner at the first intersection, I saw tables outside a café; people were seated there, eating what looked like eggs and thick bacon and drinking coffee. The smell of the food was almost debilitating. My stomach was growling and churning from the lack of food, and probably too much liquid intake from the night before, lest aside from the salty seawater I probably ingested as well; I was starving. Only whispers and surprise glances were relinquished, but I moved forward anyway, slowly, concentrating on looking as if I hadn't just washed up on a beach, trying not to be too distracted by the smell of the food and coffee, while my thoughts ran from point to point...

"The boat was a charter, but was owned by some guy in Tampa. What a price for adventure," I thought, still not sure where I was going or what was exactly happening, or what had happened to Julie.

San Pedro, Ambergris Caye, Welcome to Paradise, the sign read. It hung by two rusty nails on the side wall of a hardware store. I jumped in the air and yelled out like I had just won the lottery before even realizing it. At least I knew where I was. "Okay, that's one piece of the puzzle," I thought, and felt even more confident now.

The people of the island were friendly and appeared to be trusting and courteous toward me, an American who looked like he had been through hell and back. Still walking along the store fronts, trying in my mind to put together the events that had landed me on this island, it suddenly occurred to me, at least part of what happened. It had all started with a late night dinner, a perfect evening with prime rib and a 1978 bottle of chardonnay from a New York winery, given to us by a friend five years earlier. "That's it!" I said out loud again; this time people turned and gave me strange and curious looks. "That must have been when whatever happened occurred," I mumbled again to myself. This had been the strangest adventure yet.

Walking over to a table, I sat down feeling relieved but exhausted, and tried again to ignore the crowd. Julie and I had met in college over a game of ping-pong at the student life center at Jeff State Jr. College, just outside Birmingham. We had been friends for years before marrying in 1992.

The idea of escaping the stress and pointless endurance of city life and corporate ladders to the warm sandy beaches of a Central American island just off the coast of Belize had been a topic of conversation ever since my consulting company was bought out by some German investors who thought their segway into the business of corporate consulting was to buyout a small to medium size firm. We had built the business over the last ten years, leaning heavily on the marketing expertise of friends and colleagues, structuring their compensation and investment in the firm with stock options and shares of the company. So, when Julie and I were contacted by the buyout guru from New York, about the aspects of selling the company to an outside entity, we were confusingly excited, but found ourselves with a golden opportunity. We called a meeting of investors and colleagues, and presented the proposal, and left the decision with them. Another week went by, and the corporate head-hunter was pressuring us for an indication of an answer. That's when Julie came up with the idea for a weekend retreat at the Grove Park Inn, a favorite place of ours as well as many of our friends and colleagues. We had to get at the heart of the matter, and either decided to accept the offer, or turn it down and plan a course of action for the next year. The offer was too big and too good to refuse. The big thing was that nobody wanted to be the first to show that expression. The sale of the company had enabled us to make this trip, and so began our journey of adventure and mystery.

There were three couples altogether, all of us friends from school or work who shared the same idea. The proceeds from the sale of the company and the stock options that had been negotiated as part of the deal, afforded the fulfillment of a dream. We all had agreed to meet on the island. The arrival date had been set for March 12, a full week after each couple's departure. Each couple had decided to travel separately, either by boat or by plane and had agreed to meet on Ambergris Cay.

The cafe, *Juan's*, was located just off the square of the tiny village, and across from an old Catholic Church that looked like it had stood there for a hundred years or more. My mind was racing; panic hit yet again. "Julie, where was Julie?" The young girl waiting tables brought a glass of chilled water, no ice. I drank it without stopping, then, feeling a bit conspicuous for gulping down the water, I apologized. The young girl stood there, as if waiting for my next request. I asked for more water, and she scurried off behind a curtain.

When the young girl returned, I asked if she had seen an American woman, about 5'6", short brown hair, medium complexion, British accent. "No, Senor'," she replied, turned to walk away, but stopped to inquire if anything else was needed. "Yes," I replied, "more water please, and something to nibble on." She smiled and disappeared into the back of the café.

"Senor'", a voice from behind me came, "Senor, I have seen an American woman." It was another waiter who had come from inside the café. I just sat there, as if everything was in slow motion, watching every step the waiter made toward me, hearing every word in slow motion as well. "Where; When?" I replied. "Last night," the waiter explained. "She came by looking for her husband. She said something about having sailed here from Galveston. She had brown hair and was so high," indicating her height with his hand."

"Which direction did she go? Did she say?" I asked desperately.

"No Senor' she did not. Perhaps you might check at the church." The waiter pointed across the street. Immediately I ran across the street to the church, my heart was pounding with anticipation.

Out of breath, I stopped for a second in front of the doors of the church, with one hand outstretched and somewhat leaning on the door to rest a minute. The doors were old and weathered, daunting and reverent. The outside structure of the church was made of stucco and had been colorfully accented, but now was long faded by the sun. Children were playing in the courtyard just outside the front entrance.

As I eased through the huge bulky doors, my eyes searching from side to side, I walked into the vestibule, and squinted to see. Someone was praying near the front. The sunlight shone through the stain glass of the church and made it difficult to see clearly. I made my way slowly toward the front of the church, walking slowly down the aisle. I had a rush of emotions. I felt awkward being in a church, as if I were a kid and was somewhere that I shouldn't be, while at the same time, I felt a rush of hope and anxiety. The figure I was looking at, trying to focus on, appeared to be a female with long dark hair. Could it be Julie? "Julie" I whispered. "Julie, is that you?"

"Ethan, Ethan," she said as she turned and ran toward me. "Where have you been? What happened to you? Are you OK?" she said in her slight English accent. She had grown up in Cheshire, England, but at the age of 18, had moved to Birmingham, Alabama, to live with an uncle, Jim Buchanan who was in politics at the time, serving as a United States Senator from Alabama.

"I'm fine. I'm Ok." I told her. Then, we just stood there, holding each other until we both regained our composure and were breathing a bit easier. We kissed, and tears filled both our eyes. "Ethan, I thought you were..." She couldn't finish her sentence. I gently stroked her hair, and calmed her by placing his finger to her lips, and whispering,

"Shh, Shh, I'm here. And, you're here. That's all that matters right now. I love you so much." Then, I kissed her gently on the lips, and we held each other again.

"Come on," I motioned, leading her by the hand, "Let's go over here and talk and get our thoughts together."

We went to the side of the church, at the end of a pew, sat down and began to try to put together the pieces of what had happened. With the sun beaming in their eyes through the stain glass windows of the church, we sat for a minute, silent, motionless, both contemplating what had happened and what would come next.

"Come on. Let's go over to Juan's cafe. I need some food, and some air. Besides, I can't think here. It's too reverent of a place," I said in a low whispering voice. Julie smiled, took my hand, and nodded her head in agreement. We left the church and headed for the café.

Sitting at a small side table, back at the street side café, we collected ourselves and began to reconstruct the events of the last evening, as I motioned to the young girl who had waited on me before...right after I had asked her to bring out some munchies. The girl smiled, disappeared, only to reappear with a large plate topped with cheese and chicken nachos.

*** *** *** *** *** ***

Carl was in disbelief, sitting at the edge of his seat. Good thing he had plenty of help on this cool morning. In the span of about 45 minutes, several people, mostly college students, had filtered in and made themselves comfortable on one of the many leather sofas situated in the coffee café'. Carl had worked hard for the little piece of the American dream. He didn't make much money, but he had a connection in Jamaica where he was able to procure a plentiful supply of Blue Mountain Coffee, some of the best coffee in the world, rival only to the pure Kona coffee from Hawaii. "I need to put this in my blog, Ethan. It could potentially be a money maker you know." Carl said. He was always looking for a way to make a buck, and enhance his business.

"I thought blogs were for politicos," I said, responding to Carl's seemingly exuberant interest in our story.

"I need another mocha java, Carl, if we're going to get to a stopping point in this story."

With that and a motion to one of the girls working behind the counter, a fresh large cup of Carl's famous mocha java arrived at our table. And, as usual, it was delicious.

Chapter Three

We rented a boat out of Galveston Bay, Texas. It was a sailing ship, complete with the basic crew, and the look of a 19th century schooner. The captain and four crew-members had assured us that the journey would be safe and enjoyable, as we embarked on our plan of moving to an island for a year. More than ten years developing the company and building the business, and its subsequent sale had paid off; we were making a concerted effort to simplify our lives by giving up the daily grind of big city life in Atlanta, for the more relaxed and meager lifestyle of island living. We had paid off all of our debts, sold our house in Virginia Highlands, a very eclectic neighborhood near the downtown area of Atlanta, and all but one car, although we had kept our townhouse in Asheville, for our return and re-entry back to the civilized world. With $50,000 to fund our adventure for the next year, and trusting our other investments with Mike, a friend and also a former college pal, who happened to work in the banking and financial services business, we set out on our journey, leaving Atlanta and its horrendous road-rage traffic behind. The plan included utilizing my background in construction, teaching, and working with large groups in the corporate world, to pave the way for the next year. Beyond that, we would fly by the seat of our pants, as the saying goes. Point being, we had no definitive plan, and it was by design.

Meanwhile, back at Juan's café, Julie and I gather our thoughts. Aside from Julie still wearing the clothes from the night before, and looking a little windblown, whom really didn't stand out from the crowd, we sat as we waited for our food and coffee, as if nothing much had happened. My clothes, on the other hand, looked as though I had been in a fight with a cat. The sleeves of my shirt were torn and shredded; my pants had been soaked, dried, soaked and dried again, and had that week old look. I felt probably much better than I looked. I just kept my focus, and didn't make eye contact. Besides, if I were to describe what I had just been through, no one would believe it, and most pointed, we still had a mystery to figure out.

"What do you remember, Julie?" I asked as we sipped our coffee.

"I don't remember, exactly," speaking with her English accent. "I was awakened this morning by the noise of the children playing near the church. I guess I had fallen asleep there, but I just don't remember everything. The morning sun was so bright and it became warm very quickly, so I went into the church to stay cool and collect my thoughts. Oh,

Ethan, I was so frightened," Julie said, still looking worried.

"I know, darling, I know. So was I. But I was more confused than anything else."

As we finished the eggs and bacon, and drank yet another cup of coffee, we felt more confident about the ability to get ourselves settled and taken care of. We telephoned Mike at the bank in Atlanta and arranged for a money wire, as Juan, the owner of the café, who had befriended us, agreed to assist with the money transfer. We would hang out for the rest of the day until we could secure the money. Juan had remembered us from a previous trip to Belize, which was a lucky break for us, as we were, at least for the moment, literally stranded with no money, no I.D., and in a foreign country, all on the cusp of a mysterious event.

We went back to the public pier and snooped around for clues and the whereabouts of the other couples who had joined us on this adventure. As far as we knew, they had not yet arrived.

Belize was a place we all had been before and were comfortable mingling with the native and local people. We were also familiar with the island, and knew where to look for a safe and inconspicuous place to stay where we would not necessarily be noticed, and could blend in with the other tourist. This was not an isolated country or island. It had been a diver's paradise since the early 1960s, and only recently had the island become a semi-popular tourist adventure destination; however, it still offered unique hideaway spots for those who wished to escape the world of hustle and bustle.

The public pier was located about a quarter mile south of the church and café where we had found each other and had breakfast. We walked as casually as we could, trying not to cause unnecessary notice. We were not yet sure whom our enemies were or whom to trust.

The pier was about 22 feet wide and made of wide weather-dried planks. Several fishing boats and two rather large dive rigs were moored to the dock posts, tied with large grass ropes worn smooth by many years of use in this semi-tropical climate. To the left of the entrance of the pier was the public rental office, complete with a counter where shirtless men with their tanned leathery skin stood talking and laughing, while on the opposite side of the counter, a guy was checking the dive schedules for the morning and afternoon dives. Multicolored air tanks lined the wall and a diver flag was draped across the top of the window.

"My God, Martha Stewart would flip," Julie mumbled, looking at the décor.

"May I help you?" A voice came from the corner across the room. He was a rather young looking fellow: an American, light brown hair and tanned skin, with a slim built.

"Ah, yes, ah, I mean, we're just looking around; killing a little time," I answered without making eye-contact, trying to stay cool and collected, which was perhaps rather foolish on my part since my pants were ripped from the thigh down to about his ankles on one leg, and the other was ripped just as badly, but shorter. Julie's hair looked like a seagull had roosted overnight, and our faces, arms and other exposed parts of our bodies were dirty from the night we had just gone through.

Rolling her eyes slightly, Julie glanced in my direction, as though thinking how I always tried to be the knight in shining armor. This was an odd situation. Julie glanced over at the young man in the corner, the same one who had just asked if he could be of any help.

Without hesitating, and to my dismay albeit momentary (I have such faith in Julie's ability to fend for herself; she is a very independent woman, full of tenacity and with fearless nerves.) She charged forward with her direct inquiry.

"Well actually, yes, we were wondering what you charge for dive trips," she imposed. "The charge rates are posted on the board behind you," the young man quipped, indicating with a glance rather than fully pointed directly with his hand or finger. He seemed amused, and of course, looked as he was sizing us up, or at the very least, wondering where we had washed up from. We did look pretty wild!

Without moving her body, she slightly turned her head toward the board in question, and then smiled just ever so slightly, "Oh, yes, I see;" the rates were $45.00 per hour, plus equipment, lunch provided on morning dives; night dives -- $75.00 per hour, no food, water only provided; equipment rental - $35.00 per day; experienced divers only! "Yes, well, (toning down her English accent) we would be interested in a little snorkeling. Do you provide that service?"

"No. Sorry." An awkward pause, and suddenly things felt very conspicuous, so we said thank you and turned and left.

"What was that all about?" I asked in a soft voice as we made our way down the dock, posing as casual tourists who were just looking around.

"Ethan, the only way we are going to find out about the others is to make contact with somebody whom we might be able to trust, if only for a little bit."

"I know (feeling kind of stupid), but...I don't know, let's keep walking and maybe we'll figure this out." My thoughts and mind was raced from one scenario to another. We definitely had hit our second wind.

As we walked toward the end of the pier, we noticed a vessel docked at the very end, with three very tall masts. We stopped, looked at each other, then began to look and walk eagerly toward the boat, trying to figure out if this was the boat we had rented and boarded out of Galveston Bay. It was tied off next to a large fishing boat; one that obviously would be rented for deep sea fishing. "There, look!" I said, holding onto Julie's hand. Julie stood silent. *~MISS SHIELA~* the name of the boat, printed in large blue lettering on the stern of the boat.

"I'll just be doggoned," I said. "Look at this. Is this not a surprise?"

"Check it out, Ethan, make sure there isn't anyone around," Julie said as she glanced behind her.

It was the same boat we had sailed on. Suddenly, a cold chill ran up our backs. Without saying anything, we both turned and began walking back toward the entrance of the pier.

"Don't look anxious, Julie, let's just act normal. Maybe we can get out of here without being noticed by anyone. I wonder where the captain and his four idiot-mates are."

"I don't know, darling, but this would make a great book. Nobody would believe us if we were to phone home and tell them. Oh, jolly right, we're having a bloody blast down here amongst the fish and the sea. It's a real Moby Dick story, alright!"

"Julie, let's just get the heck out of here." I said with a determined but low voice.

"Yeah, right; let's go."

Chapter Four

Rounding the end of the pier and back on the gravel road, we turned left, headed south toward the *Victoria House*, a quaint place where we had previously stayed. We slowed to a more relaxed walk, feeling a bit less threatened and worried. What we had seen on the wharf, where the boat we had sailed on, was to say the least, unnerving. As we walked, we both realized that we both were in a trance of thought, and almost simultaneously, we both looked at each other and took a deep breath, as if to signal that it was time to compare notes. The walk from the center of San Pedro to the Victoria House took about thirty minutes. It was a clean and fairly inexpensive place to stay, and would have good, safe food to eat. Besides, we had been in contact with the innkeeper about possibly staying there a few nights until we could get our place set-up. We had secured the rental of a house not far from the Victoria House. The inn would also have a record of our stays in the past and, would let us stay the night based on our word of promise of payment after the money transfer was received by wire at the café.

Luck had finally smiled our way. Leonardo, the manager on duty at the check-in desk had remembered speaking with me three weeks before about lodging arrangements. And, as we had hoped, we were given a room, actually a one-room grass hut, which had a small stove, sink, one bed, a shower, and a couple of sitting chairs; no air conditioner, which was fine with Julie and me. We were just glad to have a base from which to operate. Leonardo also agreed to send for some clothes, since his sister worked at one of the local island clothing stores. We gave him our sizes, and he promised to return shortly with at least one set of fresh clothing for each of us. For now, we would settle for a cold shower, some lunch and a margarita for Julie and a cold beer for me. We knew it would take Leonardo about an hour to return with our newly acquired clothes. We undressed and took advantage of the roomy shower, and the opportunity for a little soapy pleasure as well.

We were asleep on the bed, each barely covered by the towels we used to dry with, when Leonardo returned with a plastic bag filled with clothes.

"Senor Ethan, Ms. Julie, you in there?" he asked as he rapped on the door of the grass hut.

"Yes, Leonardo, just a minute," still groggy from sleep, I threw the bed cover over Julie, who hadn't heard the knock on the door, grabbed my pants, hurriedly slipped them on, and answered the door.

"Leonardo thanks. Were you able to get us some clothes?"

"Oh yes, my sister had plenty. She said for you and Ms. Julie to come by and she would give you more. You can pay her later, Mon; your word is good here."

"Thanks again Leonardo, you'll never know how much I appreciate this."

"No problem. The evening meal will be ready in about an hour. What do you and the Ms. Julie want for dinner?" Leonardo said is his heavy Caribbean-Spanish accent.

"Ah, Leonardo, surprise us. We'll eat anything at this point."

With the bag of clothes in hand, I waved as Leonardo made his way back toward the main building, and Julie had gotten up and was moving toward the shower again. I waited this time, and then showered again myself.

Our table was waiting, complete with candle, a bottle of wine, and bowl of iced shrimp for a quick and satisfying appetizer. Our meal had been specially prepared. Crab cakes and stuffed shrimp initiated the evening, followed by blackened flounder, steamed oysters, black beans and rice. Finally, we were feeling rejuvenated.

We ate until nothing was left, thanked everyone, and excused ourselves from the dining area. When we had walked a sufficient distance, far enough not to be heard, we found one of the hammocks and sat listening to the ocean waves, and contemplating our next move.

"Where do you suppose the others are?" Julie whispered. "And we haven't yet fully put the pieces together from last night. What do you think happened?"

"Yes, I know. The last thing I remember was the party. We were all on the forward deck, along with the other folks who had booked their trips to parts of Mexico and beyond. You know, the wine seemed awfully strong."

"Yes, it did. And, that really seems to be the last thoughts I remember as well," Julie noted, leaning back in the hammock. "I remember chatting with Sarah, the lady from Seattle, about her trips to Honduras. And from there, my memory is quite fuzzy. Is that your sense too, darling?" Julie added.

"Do you suppose that the captain and the four idiots got us drunk enough so that we passed out, then took our money and threw us overboard?"

"Darling, Ethan. That would sort of make sense. The guy with the scar on his face was flirting with me; I do remember that. And he was very inquisitive as to how we would manage living on the island."

"Sorry dear, I didn't see him doing that. Was he being a lush about it?"

"No, he was sly about his inquiry, but that angle makes perfect sense the more I think about it."

"Well, we have to locate the others tomorrow. I heard Leonardo talking about tomorrow being

Thursday. We left Galveston Bay on Monday, and had planned to take three days to sail here. The others weren't leaving until Tuesday, so that would have been yesterday."

"Right; that would put them arriving perhaps tomorrow." Julie looked worried and perplexed.

"Ethan, we should check out the docks again. What if the captain and his cronies have plans for the others? And, there's no way to reach them by cell phone; there's no way to warn them."

"You're right, darling. Perhaps we should sneak away later to have a look, after everyone has gone to bed. We have to be very cautious."

"Ok. But, how much did you tell Leonardo about having no money and the state of disarray we were in when we arrived; is there any possibility he suspects anything?" Julie asked, being careful to whisper.

"Can't be certain," I said. "I told Leonardo that we had been fishing and lost our wallets, and that our luggage had not arrived yet."

"Did he buy it?" Julie inquired, glancing around as she spoke because there were other couples walking close by.

"He seemed to have, but at this point we can't trust anyone."

"Right; let's wait awhile, and then we can go. Besides, I'm exhausted," Julie said, holding and gently stroking my arm. The steady clanking of diesel engines could be heard in the distance and the air was cool with a slight breeze. The ache in my shoulders felt as though my muscles were tied in square knots. Julie's head lay on my shoulder and her left leg was dangling from the side of the hammock. We had fallen asleep. I looked at my watch, but, of course, it wasn't there. I had forgotten. The sky was filled with bright stars against a deep purplish blue background; there were no clouds to be seen. The clanking noise I had heard earlier was that of the engines of the shrimp boats easing their way out from the protected waters, as the silhouette of a freighter inched silently across the horizon.

"Julie," I whispered. "Julie, wake up. We've missed it, I'm afraid."

"What?" She mumbled as she too began to realize that her neck and shoulders were stiff as a dried rope.

"What time is it?" she asked. "I don't know; remember, I lost my watch somewhere in the night."

"Oh yes, that's right. Is it too late to go search and snoop around?"

"Do you really want to go now? It seems late. Besides, I don't want Leonardo or any of the other workers to suspect what we're doing. And since we haven't moved from this hammock for hours, let's just go to our hut and crash. I think I'll need more amours in the morning."

"O.K. darling, you talked me into it, but I'll be worried about the others if they don't show by tomorrow." Julie climbed out of the hammock first, and then began to pull on my hand.

"Yes, well, so will I; come on, let's go," I replied in a low voice as we started walking toward our hut.

~ Football Town ~

About the Author:

Born in 1957, near Bessemer, Alabama, Dr. Hale now resides in Savannah, Georgia, with his wife of almost 30 years. Hale has two children, and five grandchildren. Hale has traveled all across the United States, the Caribbean, Central America, and British West Indies. He has lived and worked in Georgia, Alabama, and Texas. His rural roots and meager beginnings, along with his life experiences, provide the source for his imaginative stories and characters. He attended small schools, lived and worked in a small community, and grew up cheering for the University of Alabama and Bear Bryant, and spent many Saturday afternoons at the renown Legend Field, near downtown Birmingham.

He completed his Doctorate in Educational Leadership in1999 at Vanderbilt University. Previously, Dr. Hale also earned a Bachelor's, Degree, Masters Degree, and Specialists Degree, all in areas of education. He served as a teacher, coach, middle school and high school principal, and superintendent, before returning to the classroom as a fourth grade teacher for students with special needs.

In 2006, Hale played the role of Judge Fort, in an independent film based in Birmingham, Alabama, about the story and case of Edwin Stevenson and the murder of Father James Coyle. Stevenson was defended by Hugo Black, then a highly renowned defense attorney, who later became a U.S. Senator from Alabama, and who eventually was appointed to the U.S. Supreme Court.

Hale currently teaches 5th grade inclusion at Bloomingdale Elementary, in Bloomingdale, Georgia, near Savannah, Georgia.

www.ingramcontent.com/pod-product-compliance
Lightning Source LLC
LaVergne TN
LVHW011218080426
835509LV00005B/200